Why I Hate the Yankees

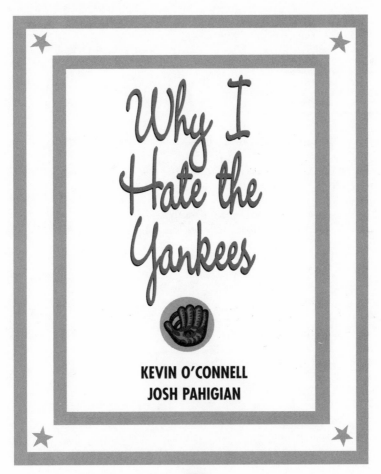

Why I Hate the Yankees

KEVIN O'CONNELL

JOSH PAHIGIAN

The Lyons Press
Guilford, Connecticut
An imprint of The Globe Pequot Press

The Lyons Press is an imprint of The Globe Pequot Press.

10 9 8 7 6 5 4 3 2 1

Printed in the United States of America

Library of Congress Cataloging-in-Publication Data
O'Connell, Kevin.
  Why I hate the Yankees / by Kevin O'Connell & Josh Pahigian.
      p. cm.
  Includes bibliographical references.
  ISBN 1-59228-763-8 (trade paper)
  1. New York Yankees (Baseball team)—Miscellanea. 2. New York Yankees (Baseball
team)—Humor. I. Pahigian, Josh. II. Title.
GV875.N4O36 2005
796.357'64'097471—dc22

                              2005022510

Contents

Authors' Introduction vii

One   Yankee Baseball, Yankee Business 3

Two   Family Ties: One Family's Contentious Baseball History 19

Three   George Steinbrenner: The Man, The Myth, The Felon 25

Four   Trader Josh 37

Five   Over-Played, Over-Hyped, Overrated 41

Six   Film Review: *Damn Yankees* 55

Seven   Yankee Fans—Just What Makes 'em Tick 63

Eight   The Sad Case of Mr. Salvo 79

Nine   Yankee Pride, Yankee Arrogance 85

Ten   No Day at the Ballpark 101

Eleven   The Axis of Baseball Evil—It Wasn't Always This Way 107

Twelve   The Yankees Always Get You in the End 121

Thirteen   The Yankee Mystique—The Mystery Unraveled 127

Fourteen   Into the Heart of Darkness 141

Fifteen   Yankee Imperialism 153

Sixteen   The Greedy Glutton's Curse 169

Seventeen   An Open Letter to Yankee Fans........................ 177
Eighteen   An Open Letter to George Steinbrenner................ 191
            Bibliography.. 201
            Acknowledgments 205
            About the Authors 207

vi

Hating the Yankees is as American as
pizza pie, unwed mothers, and cheating on
your income tax.
—Mike Royko

Before you read about our mutual hatred of the New York Yankees, we thought it might be useful to tell you a little bit about who we are and why we decided to write this book.

First off, "hate" is a very strong word, and we want to make it clear that we're not two people who ordinarily use a rancorous word like "hate" lightly. In the course of our daily lives, we both try to abide by all of the principles that generally make it possible for a society to function in relative harmony. Whenever possible, we do unto others as we'd like them to do unto us; we give folks we don't know the benefit of the doubt; we try not to pee in the shower at the gym; we don't wrestle foul balls away from little kids (at least Kevin doesn't); and so forth.

To put it another way, if life were a baseball game and Kevin were a base runner barreling into second base trying to break up a double play, he would slide in hard, but he would slide in straight, taking aim directly at the base, not toward the shortstop who had

> Rooting for the Yankees is like rooting for U.S. Steel.
> —Joe. E. Lewis

already sidestepped five feet toward right-center field. And if Josh were a batter who'd just taken a fastball on the shoulder, rather than charge the mound, he'd put his head down, trot to first base, brush himself off, and vow to knock a base hit back through the box his next time up.

> **KEVIN:** Like a pitcher would actually bother to brush you back.
> **JOSH:** You haven't stolen a bag since Little League.

When it comes to baseball, first and foremost we are fans of the game. Before such important matters as team loyalties, favorite players, and favorite ballparks arise, we respect the game and athletes who play it at all levels, especially those few talented enough to play in the big leagues. We love the drama, the strategy, and the pure genius of the greatest sport ever invented. We love the one-on-one confrontation between pitcher and batter. We love the grace and beauty of a diving catch in the outfield grass. We love the "thwack" of a collision at home plate. We love tracking OPS percentages, lefty-righty splits, WHIP ratios, and Holds. Heck, we even love rain delays, as long as the concession stands are well stocked with beer and hot cocoa.

The truth is, we love this game so much that in 2003 we quit our jobs and left our wonderful wives home alone for three months to make the pilgrimage to all thirty major league ballparks. We had a blast and even wrote a book about our experiences—*The Ultimate Baseball Road Trip*—after grudgingly returning to our normal lives. Like a lot of folks, when it comes to baseball, we're hard core.

Inevitably when people feel strongly about something—be it baseball, their country, or even Swedish rock bands—and they see someone else mistreating that thing, enemies are born. It's the way of the world. We're baseball fans, and we happen to think the Yankees are bad for baseball. And after you hear everything we have to say, we think you'll agree with us. But if you don't, we won't exactly lose any sleep over the matter. After all, our primary mission in writing this book is not to make friends with everyone in baseball, but rather to do our part to preserve all that we find good and true about the National Pastime.

That said, we can safely say without hesitation that we HATE the Yankees . . . and Bud Selig. We REALLY HATE them. We hate the Yankees and Bud Selig because we believe that both are bad for baseball. This book is about our hatred of the Yankees, so we will try to consider Bud Selig another topic for another day. In truth, our hatred of the Bronx Bombers runs much deeper than our hatred of the commissioner. And here's why. Selig may be bumbling and misguided, and his entire commissionership may have been based upon an enormous conflict of interest during those seven years when he was both the commish and the de facto owner of the Brewers, but we believe that in his heart his decisions and actions have always been based upon what he thinks is best for the game. For example, Bud thought that it was good for attendance if batters hit a lot of home runs—really absurdly long home runs—so he agreed to a five-strikes-and-you're-out (for one year) steroid policy as part of the 2002 collective bargaining agreement. Turns out Bud's agreement had about as much teeth to it as the average guest on *The Jerry Springer Show*. But we can't deny that Bud based this policy on what *he thought* was best for the game. We just didn't happen to agree with him and

> The majority of American males put themselves to sleep by striking out the batting order of the New York Yankees.
> —James Thurber

neither did a whole lot of other fans; that's why baseball and the Players Association were forced to come up with a new, stricter anti-doping policy early in 2005.

The Yankees, on the other hand, cannot be written off as bumbling stooges, and the decisions their leader makes are never based on what he perceives to be in the best interests of the game. George Steinbrenner is acutely aware that what is good for the Yankees is often very bad for baseball as a whole. But he doesn't care a lick. As he likes to remind folks, he's built his entire life and career upon the simple philosophy: "Winning is the most important thing, after breathing. Breathing first, winning next." Notice there's no mention of ethics or fair play in George's little mantra.

Do we hate George Steinbrenner for wanting to win?

Of course not. We're all baseball fans, and we all want our teams to win. We don't hate the Yankees because they have won more championships than any other two major league teams combined. Well, perhaps we do hate them for that, just a little bit. But that's not the major reason for our distaste for all things Yankee. We believe that every professional ball club, just like every individual in this country, is entitled to strive to be the very best. That's the American way, and who are we to knock the American way? Our hatred of the Yankees has less to do with the fact that the Yankees win and more to do with how they win because, as our book will make clear, the Yankees' success comes at the expense of not only the other twenty-nine teams, but at the expense of the very league itself.

In the course of this book, we'll try to explain how each of the following undeniable truths reflects on just how significantly the Yankees are crippling the viability of baseball:

- The Yankees win by spending more money than other teams . . . way, way more.

- The Yankees win while receiving preferential treatment from the league and media.
- The Yankees win while being as arrogant and selfish as they want to be.
- Alex Rodriguez is a metrosexual, pretty-boy punk.

But before we get into specifics such as these, there is still the matter of who we, your authors, happen to be. Here is a bit more about us.

Kevin grew up in the Pacific Northwest, pitching and playing first base for his youth baseball teams, and riding a lot of pine for his Babe Ruth team. Growing to six foot five gave him the frame of a basketball player, not a baseball player, no matter how great his desire was to play in the big leagues. Fact: Kevin's father, the man who taught him to read the box scores, catch flies, and hang the curve ball much too high in the strike zone, was, and still is, an ardent Yankees fan.

Meanwhile, Josh grew up in Massachusetts, playing a less-than-mediocre third base for his youth and middle school teams. After taking a grounder to the teeth in ninth grade, he was relegated to playing a less-than-mediocre right field where the potential for injury was significantly diminished. Fact: Josh's father was, and still is, a diehard Red Sox fan, which, by definition, makes Josh a dyed-in-the-wool, card-carrying Yankee-hater.

In short, Kevin grew up about as far away from New York City as someone can while still having his feet planted within the

It doesn't feel any different being here [at the All-Star Game]. I feel like I'm on an All-Star team everyday.
—Derek Jeter

> The only problem with success is that it does not teach you how to deal with failure.
> —Tommy Lasorda

perimeter of the Major League Baseball universe, while Josh grew up just three hours north of Yankee Stadium. Kevin was raised in a household where Yankee Pride was highly respected, while Josh was raised in a home where family members were required to spit after mentioning the name of any Yankee player. Despite these differences, both became fervent Yankee-haters. Coincidence? Not a chance. There are literally hundreds of millions of Yankee-hating folks just like us throughout this country and around the world. Most of us Yankee-haters live productive lives, raise kind and generous families, and grow weary every time our team is outbid for a quality free agent by the American League New York franchise. We're mad as hell and getting madder, and we have a few things to say about the matter.

Now, we realize that in most cases baseball loyalties, like political party affiliations, run deep in family bloodlines, being passed down from one generation to the next. This we cannot deny. But we also can't deny that in the life of an intelligent, observant person there naturally comes a time when he or she questions whether it is right to vote the way mom or dad do. There comes a time in every young republican's life when he realizes that he is an individual, capable of making his own choices, and considers voting democrat. That doesn't

> Hating the Yankees isn't part of my act. It is one of those exquisite times when life and art are in perfect conjunction.
> —Former Chicago White Sox owner Bill Veeck

mean he always does it, but he at least brings something of an open mind to the voting booth. Clearly Kevin did this when he chose to root against his father's Yankees. And while Josh may have been predestined to be another Pahigian Red

Sox–rooter, he'd like to think that even if he had been born in Connecticut or New York, he'd have identified more closely with the Red Sox or another team, rather than with the Yankees, for reasons related to his morals and values.

In any case, as we sat down together to write this book, we cannot say that we brought no personal biases to our keyboards. If that were the case and we were entirely objective, what kind of baseball fans would we be? In a word: inauthentic—the worst kind of fans. After all, baseball breeds deep loyalties—or at least it should. That's what makes the game and its fans so interesting.

We'd also like to offer a few words, if we might, to those Yankee fans reading this Introduction who may have gotten this book as a gag gift in their Christmas stocking or at their bat mitzvah party: Remember, we're just the messengers. Don't get any big ideas about dumping beer on us if you see us at a ball game. Relax, and try to enjoy the book in the spirit in which it was written. The joke is on you here, so deal with it with grace. Let your slew of championship trophies console you.

Finally, we want everyone to understand that we don't *want* to hate anyone, not even George Steinbrenner, the Yankees' players, or the Yankees' fans. We want to get along with all people, especially baseball fans. We can only hope that our book inspires The Big Stein and all of the budding Little Steins out there to realize that it is nobler to build championship teams from the ground up than it is to merely buy them, that a little bit of modesty can go a long way, and that what's good for the Yankees isn't always what's best for baseball as a whole. Long live the National Pastime.

Sincerely,

YOUR AUTHORS, KEVIN AND JOSH

> George Steinbrenner is the center of evil in the universe.
> —Ben Affleck

Why I Hate the Yankees

Chapter One

Yankee Baseball, Yankee Business

Since winning their first World Championship in 1923, the New York Yankees have never stopped racking up titles. The Yanks entered the 2005 season with twenty-six World Series wins under their collective pinstriped belt, while the next closest team, the St. Louis Cardinals, had garnered only nine. That means the Yankees have been nearly three times as successful as the next best team in baseball. And the Yankees are all too happy to remind the rest of the baseball world just how magnificent they are. The team hangs World Series banners around Yankee Stadium like Josh's college roommate used to hang centerfold pin-ups around their dorm room.

Not only do the Yanks often win it all, but even when they don't they usually make it to the World Series—or at least go deep into the playoffs. You can count on the Yankees playing baseball in October just like you can count on the Dallas Cowboys playing football on

> It's very difficult to bid against a team that has an unlimited budget. It doesn't matter how many outfielders or how many starters they already have, with an unlimited budget you can buy anyone you think you need.
> —John W. Henry, Boston Red Sox owner

Thanksgiving Day. Barring a catastrophic event, it's a given. Between 1921 and 2004, the Yankees played in forty of the eighty-three World Series championships. Pretty remarkable stuff, huh? In a league that has grown to encompass thirty teams and to incorporate two playoff rounds that teams must overcome just to get to the World Series, the Yankees have continued to be *that* dominant. They've been consistent too. It's not like they had one remarkable stretch. The Yanks have won in every era of the game's history. From the "Murderers' Row" Yankees of the late 1920s, to the Lou Gehrig–led four-time World Series champs of 1936–1939, to Casey Stengel's five-peat winners of 1949–1953, to the Whitey Ford–inspired teams that appeared in five straight October Classics in 1960–1964, to the Bronx Zoo champions of 1977 and 1978, to Joe Torre's three-peat champs of 1998–2000, the Yanks have been winners. That unsuccessful stretch between 1979 and 1996 when the Yanks won no titles, well, we like to call those years our "glory days."

JOSH: I long for the days when Steve Sax and Alvaro Espinoza anchored the middle infield for the Yanks.
KEVIN: And I, for the days when Oscar Azocar, Roberto Kelly, and Jesse Barfield graced, or should I say blighted, the Yankee outfield.

JOSH: Oscar Azocar. That's a name I'd forgotten.

KEVIN: And a name plenty of Yankee fans would like to forget too.

The fact is, other than that unsuccessful stretch, the Yankees have consistently won. They won in the earliest days of the live ball, when the pitcher's mound was high, after the mound was lowered, before free agency, after free agency, before the players were using steroids and while the players were using steroids. Heck, they even won the World Series in 1943 when Joe DiMaggio and the rest of the team's stars were off fighting World War II. Even New York's replacement players were better than the other teams' replacement players.

Here's a startling confession. We have no problem with the first twenty-one titles the Yankees won. No problem whatsoever.

Of course, as baseball fans we can see how it might have been better for the growth of the game nationwide had the joy of winning been a tad more evenly dispersed between 1923 and 1962 when the Yankees won twenty-one of the forty World Series played. And of course we think the game would have been better off without many of New York's arrogant drunken players who set poor examples for our nation's impressionable youth. And it is undeniable that the Yankees preyed on their economically disadvantaged baseball brethren to buy stars from other teams and, in effect, bought several of their titles. And yes, the Yankees of old also scarfed up the best amateur talent in the pre-draft era that allowed teams to bid against one another for high school, college, and minor league players.

But the situation in those old days was never as bad as it is today. Certain changes in the way the game is played—on, and particularly *off*, the field—have given today's Yankees more of a competitive advantage than ever before. The competitiveness of the game today is kind of like when Kevin coached a youth basketball team and challenged his seventh graders to play him one on one. The kids tried really hard, and a few of them could shoot fairly well, but Kevin was still a foot taller than the tallest thirteen-year-old.

KEVIN: Hmm . . . I wonder if the Devil Rays feel short when they play the Yankees.
JOSH: Maybe not short . . . but certainly slow of foot, arm speed, and bat speed . . . and less powerful.
KEVIN: That might explain Devil Ray Alex Sanchez's steroid use.
JOSH: Sure, a clear case of Yankee Envy.

Since George Steinbrenner took control of the Yankees in 1973, the team has adhered to a business strategy centered almost exclusively upon the principle of outspending other teams for top player talent. As a result, the Yankees' free-spending ways have driven player salaries higher and higher across baseball. We're guessing that George gets plenty of fruit baskets each year at Christmas time from player agents and Players Association executives. To be fair, we'll give the man his due. Despite the questionable characters with whom he has often chosen to surround himself, it is undeniable that George Steinbrenner builds winning baseball teams (if you don't count the years between 1978 and 1996). The Yankees began 2005 having won eight straight AL East titles. In their first thirty years under George's ownership—

> This is my 24th year of doing this, and the Yankees' payroll has been "dangerously high" 24 of 24. They've been the Goliath of the game, and I don't expect their position to change.
> —Scott Boras, player agent

counting the two periods when he was suspended from the game—the Yankees won five World Series. This may not seem as remarkable as some of the Yankees' previous dynasties. In fact, though, it is no small feat in an era of free agency, expansion, revenue sharing, and multitiered playoffs. The Cincinnati Reds are the only other team to have won as many as three championships since Steinbrenner took the helm of the Yanks in 1973.

Some readers might still be wondering, "What's George's winning formula?" We're guessing these are the same naïve folks who scratched their heads when they saw Anna Nicole Smith walking arm in arm with her octogenarian groom and wondered what the old-timer's "secret" was. The fact is that people with even a cursory knowledge of the way the world works know that the answer in both instances has to do with a whole lot of cash and a willingness to spend it lavishly.

Unfortunately, Anna Nicole isn't the only top-heavy floozy for hire in our society. There are plenty who belong to the male gender who also happen to be adept with a baseball bat or ball in their hands. Like a John walking through Times Square, Steinbrenner flashes his wad of cash, and the players come a-callin'. And George, well, he just can't say no.

> **KEVIN:** No names, please.
> **JOSH:** Are his initials Randy Johnson?
> **KEVIN:** I don't know who that tall, well-groomed guy on the mound for the Yanks is. Randy Johnson has pock marks and a mullet.

George is like the little boy in the candy store—or, to continue our previous analogy, the rogue sailor in the whorehouse—who wants more, more, more, and is simply out of control. He must satisfy his yearning, aching lust for elite players.

The Yankee bankroll buys players away from other teams. This compromises the competitive balance of the league and asks for more good faith of fans than they can be reasonably expected to give. Sure, it's still fun and meaningful to be a baseball fan in New York and in the other handful of cities (Boston, Chicago, Los Angeles) that offer their teams the luxury of hefty television and advertising deals. But what about the fans in the rest of the country? Each year that Steinbrenner puts a team on the field with a higher payroll than the gross national product of Ecuador and the Republic of Chad combined (don't quote us on those numbers, it's just a joke) is another year that begins with no hope for a championship in small-market towns like Kansas City, Milwaukee, Pittsburgh, Detroit, Toronto, Minneapolis, and Tampa/St. Petersburg.

The only way for these budget-conscious franchises to acquire top talent is by developing it themselves. And that, of course, takes time. First, they must make their selections wisely at each year's amateur draft. They must draft diamonds-in-the-rough—players who are talented, but not so talented that they will hire a super-agent like Scott Boras and hold out for ridiculous signing bonuses. Then they must invest several years to nurture their new players, helping them refine their skills in the minor leagues. After years of teaching these individuals, when finally the cream of the talent crop arrives in the major leagues, the teams still must be patient as their young players experience the ordinary learning curve that rookies face. After perhaps three or four years of big league play, most players begin to scratch at their athletic potential. The good news for these players is that after six years of major league service they can file for free agency and sign with the highest bidder. The bad news for the teams that scouted, drafted, signed, and patiently developed the players is that nine times out of ten, they lose their players to free agency. They are left with rosters full of young players and aging journeymen, while the rich teams, especially the Yankees, don't have to waste their time with the growing pains associated with player development.

The Yankees don't have to worry about developing players in the minor leagues. Their minor league teams play in Oakland, Baltimore, Kansas City, and any other major league town that can't afford to keep its best major leaguers as they approach free agency. Each year the Yankees carpet-bomb the free-agent market, signing more high-quality, high-priced players than they could ever put on the field at once, hoping that some combination of these poached stars will result in a winning formula.

Is it me, or was the last home-grown prospect to stick in the Yankees' locker room Jason Giambi's and Kevin Brown's intestinal parasite?
—*Sports Illustrated* writer, Bill Scheft in his column, "The Show"

The Yankees sign the best of the best free agents, stripping other teams of their marquee players. The effects are felt throughout the game. For example, for years Jason Giambi was the unshaven, burly, sweat-soaked public face of the free-wheeling Oakland A's. If anyone epitomized the wild and wooly A's, it was Giambi. Then he signed with the Yankees, got a little boy's haircut, and started hawking deodorant on TV while wearing tight-fitting J.Crew sweaters. One of the game's wildest personalities and one synonymous with the A's became just another Yankee media whore. Fans in Oakland blamed the A's for Giambi's departure, saying the team's management didn't care enough about winning to keep him. Fans across the country who had rooted for Giambi and the A's in their playoff battles against the Yankees didn't know what to think. And another chunk of the fans' faith in the system that is supposed to maintain a fair level of competitive balance was strip-mined. It seemed only fitting that Giambi admitted to using steroids to a federal Grand Jury two years later. Not only was he a sell-out, but he was a cheat as well. Apparently he had been a Yankee all along, only we hadn't been able to see through his fun-loving attitude and greasy locks.

The case of Mike Mussina offers another example of Yankee cash driving a wedge between a smaller-market team and one of its homegrown stars. Mussina came up through the Orioles' minor league system and made it to the majors in 1991 after being a first-round pick out of Stanford. Baltimore fans adored him immediately, serenading him with enthusiastic "Moose" calls whenever he took the mound. It wasn't long before he became the most identifiable player on the team. Although the Orioles of the early and mid-1990s were mediocre at best, in time the front office assembled a winning team around its ace pitcher. With fans streaming to Baltimore to see the new Oriole Park at Camden Yards and Mussina mowing down batters, the Orioles became one of the AL East's up-and-coming teams. They made the playoffs in 1996 and 1997, both times losing in the ALCS to the Yankees and Indians, respectively. As the new century dawned, a heated rivalry seemed to be brewing in the AL East between the Yanks and O's. But then Mussina became eligible for free agency, and the Yankees offered him a far more lucrative deal than Baltimore could muster. He took the money. And soon the Orioles, with their perennially young pitching staff, found themselves mired in fourth place again, in the five-team division.

> **JOSH:** Mussina is the Yankees' third starter behind Johnson and Carl Pavano.
> **KEVIN:** And the Orioles are left with a pitching rotation of . . . Moose droppings.
> **JOSH:** Not a big Sidney Ponson fan, eh?

When a player of Mussina's caliber jumps ship to join his team's fiercest enemy, it does more than leave a void on the deserted team's roster—it sends shock waves throughout the entire organization. It sends the message to the team's players and fans that their team is second rate, and that they'll never be able to maintain a consistent level of excellence because they'll never be able to compete financially with the Yankees and the handful of other large-market clubs. As the hope of winning in the city becomes less realistic, it becomes easier for other burgeoning stars on the team to also leave when their contracts expire.

In addition to dominating the free-agent market, the Yankees are not opposed to making lopsided trades to bolster their roster when the opportunity arises. Because the Yankees bid on nearly every decent free agent, other teams (competing bidders) wind up paying more than they can afford to spend on the players they are able to sign. Later, when the teams realize that they can't afford to make good on all of the large contracts they have inked, the Yankees generously bail them out. In exchange for a couple of cheap minor leaguers, or a marginal starter (usually a Yankee flameout who rode the pine in New York), the Yankees gladly undertake the burden of the big contract and the superstar who goes with it. Prior to the 2004 season, for example, the Yankees acquired Alex Rodriguez ($21,726,881 per year) from Texas, Kevin Brown ($15,714,286 per year) from Los Angeles, and Javier Vazquez ($9,000,000 per year) from Montreal. The Yankees gave up Alfonso Soriano, Jeff Weaver, and Nick Johnson, respectively, for this trio. Which three would your team rather have?

The combined salary of the three stars the Yankees acquired via trade prior to the 2004 campaign totaled $46,441,167. Add to that amount the $12,029,131 that New York handed to free agent Gary Sheffield that same off-season, and the team was on the books for four new players at $58,470,298 in 2004. To put this in perspective, the

I would only leave Boston to go back to Houston to be closer to my family. I could never come back and pitch against the Red Sox, so it would have to be in the other league. I have all the nice things in life because of the fact that [Red Sox boss] Mr. Harrington took care of me.
—then–Red Sox pitcher, Roger Clemens

He's [Steinbrenner] the one who gave me a chance to get to the World Series. This is where I wanted to be all along. We had a couple of nice offers from other teams, but I tied my agents' hands. I told them I wanted to be a Yankee.
—Roger Clemens, upon re-signing with the Yankees

These [players] are constantly moving from team to team—and they certainly have the economic right to that—and it destroys the dream that this is a permanent group of champions for your city. And that illusion is shattered every year.
—Tom Wolfe

Yanks "restocked" with four players who combined to make more than the entire twenty-five-man rosters of twelve MLB teams that season.

In addition to signing free agents and making payroll-initiated trades, there is still another player pool the Yankees exploit to stack their roster. No team has dipped into the rapidly expanding international market as aggressively as the Yankees. Because players from Cuba, Latin America, and the Asian baseball leagues are not subject to the amateur draft, they are free to sign with the highest bidder. Care to guess who that usually is? "I'll take Baseball Powermongers for $2,000, Alex!"

In recent years the Yankees have thrown tens of millions of dollars at Hideki Irabu, Orlando Hernandez, Jose Contreras, and Hideki Matsui. Never mind that Irabu (who Steinbrenner once called a "big fat pussy toad") and Contreras (who was traded to the White Sox) were total busts. The Yankees can afford to take a $28 million gamble on a live arm that might or might not pan out. They know that if they throw enough darts at the wall, one of them is bound to hit the board, like the Matsui dart did.

The difference between the Yankees and the other large-market teams is that they can spend their money freely, without the fear of being hamstrung (as other teams often are) by one or two bad signings. One needs look no farther than across town to Shea Stadium to find an example of just how devastating a few unwise long-term contracts can be to other teams. The Mets of the early 2000s gave big-time dollars to players like Roberto Alomar, Kevin Appier, and Mo Vaughn, and when they didn't produce big-time results, the team suffered mightily. At some point, the front office had to stop throwing good money after bad and ride out the bloated deals before spending more money. But such is not the case with the Yankees. They can keep pouring money on top of more money, covering up their mistakes with new players.

> Our [pitching] staff comes from all over. We have a pitcher from Cuba, a pitcher from Japan, a pitcher from Panama, and Boomer [David Wells] is from Mars.
>
> —Tino Martinez

> The Evil Empire extends its tentacles even into Latin America.
>
> —Red Sox CEO Larry Lucchino after the Red Sox lost out to the Yankees on the bidding for Jose Contreras

All of this adds up to a roster loaded with talent from top to bottom. And we do mean loaded. The 2005 Yankees became just the second team in modern baseball history to field an Opening Day lineup, including designated hitter, of former All-Stars at every single position. The only previous team to do so had been Steinbrenner's 1977 Yankees.

The reality is that most teams fill out the bottom few spots in their batting order and the last few spots on their bench with inexpensive journeymen or unproven players recently recalled from the minor leagues. Not the Yankees. They stock the twenty to twenty-five spots on their roster with aging (and still quite expensive) stars who they hand pick from other teams. Not only does this strengthen the Yankees' bench, but it also keeps quality players off the rosters of their competitors. For the Yanks, it's addition by both addition and subtraction. Veteran players like Jose Canseco, Cecil Fielder, Dwight Gooden, Daryl Strawberry, Kenny Lofton, Chili Davis, Ruben Sierra, Tim Raines, John Olerud, and David Justice come to mind as players who wore pinstripes at the tail ends of their careers, perhaps in the hopes of leaving the game with one last run at a World Series ring. The Yankees sign these players unsure of whether they might happen to need them or not. After all, when you have an All-Star at every position, you don't have too many occasions when you need a pinch-hitter. But should a starter go down with an injury or should a late inning situation arise when a heady veteran is needed, the Yankees can go to their bench knowing that their fate is in capable hands.

> **All ballplayers want to wind up their careers with the Cubs, Giants, or Yankees. They just can't help it.**
>
> **—Dizzy Dean**

It is true that baseball, in every era of its history, has had its haves and its have-nots. The best teams have always spent more money than the worst teams, and fans in losing cities have always lamented that the moneybags in the upper division had an unfair advantage. But the disparity between today's haves and have-nots has grown to an absolutely absurd level.

15

To understand how out of whack things have become, consider the 2004 season during which the Yankees spent $184 million on player salaries. The next closest payroll belonged to the Red Sox at $125 million, followed by the Angels at $101 million. After that, the figures fell off dramatically, with the mean payroll of the average major league team settling at $63 million, about a third of what the Yankees spent. The bottom five teams on the list—the Marlins, Pirates, Indians, Devil Rays, and Brewers—combined to spend a total of $172 million (still $12 million less than the Yankees).

But wait, it gets even worse. According to the terms of the 2002 labor agreement, teams spending over a certain amount each year must match—dollar for dollar—the amount by which they exceed the spending cap with a contribution to the general fund. This money is then dispersed to the small-market teams. In 2004, the Yankees exceeded the cap by $70 million, which means that after you factor in their luxury tax expenses, New York actually spent $255 million on player salaries, more than four times as much as the average team.

We say, this can't continue. Otherwise, eventually the small-market teams are going to go out of business, and the Yankees, Mets, Red Sox, Dodgers, and Angels will have nobody left to play but one another. The luxury tax was designed and implemented to slow down the Yankees' spending, but obviously it hasn't worked. After the salary-laden Yanks came up short against the Red Sox in the 2004 American League Championship Series, the team's solution was to spend, spend, spend, and spend some more in preparation for 2005. First, New York netted free-agent starting pitchers Jaret Wright and Carl Pavano, and then came the blockbuster of all blockbusters. The Yankees traded Vazquez, prospects, and $9 million in cash (surprise!) to the Diamondbacks for Randy Johnson. With the addition of The Big Unit, the Yankees' 2005 payroll soared over $204 million, and that wasn't counting the $9 million payout to Arizona or the team's projected luxury tax of nearly $85 million.

So what's a Detroit Tigers fan to do? Well, there's always fantasy baseball. No, really, we're serious. We find it more than coincidental that this modern invention has flourished while the Yankees have consumed more of the game's star players and MLB has become less competitive. Fantasy baseball gives people in cities like Detroit a reason to follow the game all season long, even if the home team is fifteen games out of first place by Memorial Day. It creates a version of the game in which every team has the same amount of money to spend on players. Thus, every team has its share of bona-fide stars, mediocre players, and scrubs.

Could it be that fantasy baseball is an evil plot invented by Steinbrenner to keep the common fan occupied while his big money dominance of the real game goes unnoticed?

Buying teams to win championships goes against everything that is sacred about sports. The entire premise of team sports is to test one team's mettle against another's on a level playing field where the rules are the same for both teams. The reason why sports have captivated so many people through the years is that the outcome of each game is not predetermined and the stakes are real and meaningful. Historically, the baseball teams that worked the hardest, overcame the most adversity, and played the best together have succeeded. And for this, they are worthy of our praise, our admiration, and our precious time in watching them. Dedication, perseverance, and teamwork are qualities most Americans can appreciate. But Old Man Steinbrenner has no time for these noble ideals. Rather than earning titles the old-fashioned way, he buys them at auction. And worst of all, we're letting him get away with it.

Chapter Two

Family Ties: One Family's Contentious Baseball History

This Yankee moment is brought to you courtesy of Kevin, his family, and the O'Connell's complicated history of baseball loyalties.

Maybe it's an Irish-Catholic thing, being feisty and rebellious by nature; I'm not completely sure. Perhaps it is simply born out of my family's love of argument, especially with one another. There seems to be no shortage of devil's advocates at the ready to challenge anyone who makes a declarative statement. Either way, our nature makes for lively baseball conversations.

In our clan, the formula, as near as I have been able to figure, goes something like this: The father *always* takes a wife that is a fan of a different team than he. Perhaps the newlyweds would be mutually bored with a spouse who agreed with the other's every word, but regardless, the contention begins at the onset of the family unit. When the first son is big enough to itch daddy's britches he, perhaps out of some deep-seeded Freudian need to best his old man, rebels against the team his father loves, and throws his support behind the father's team's arch rivals. Then the second son, being somewhat of a suck-up anyway, in his desire to please the father, aligns himself strictly with the father's team, giving the first and rebellious son twice as much intrafamily arguing as he first bargained for. After that, the younger sibs fall into line according to personality, family alliances, and so forth. And voila! Let the bickering begin.

Here's how it has played out in my family: My grandfather, Howard O'Connell, was a die-hard fan of the Bronx Bombers. Joe DiMaggio was his man: a West Coast boy who always gave his best and wasn't too flashy or full of himself—at least that's what my grandfather thought. Fair enough. Howard married Patricia McDonald, a staunch Brooklyn Dodgers fan. Their oldest son, Mike, as quick as he learned how to throw a spitball, chose to cheer for the Dodgers, even after their move to LA. He held no loyalty to any borough of NYC. Heck, to Mike, his team had moved closer to home. Then, my father, Tom O'Connell, being the second-born son, blindly followed his father and chose to support the dominant Yanks. Was he trying to get in good with the old man? Perhaps. After my father came a daughter, Kit (Dodgers fan), a son, Rick (Yankees fan), then Brian (Yankees). So you get the idea: a constant state of yelling, screaming, and people listening to different games on different radios (and then televisions) in different rooms of the house, all throughout the '40s, '50s, and into the '60s. And when the Yankees and Dodgers met in the World Series: *complete and total civil war*. I'm talking food-fights at the family dinner table, short-sheeting the beds, and running the hot water in the kitchen while other family members were showering. Nothing was taboo.

My father's devotion to the Yanks continued throughout the early years of the new hometown Seattle Mariners. So great was his reluctance to convert, in fact, that my first Major League Baseball game was the Yankees vs. Mariners, picked by my father to gleefully watch his Yankees pound the fledgling hometown expansion M's. He wore his old Yankee cap and, along with his brother Rick, drank beer in the upper deck of the Kingdome shouting, "Strike the bums out!" and "Let's Go Yankees!" They had no regard for docile and kindly Seattle fans—newbies to the grand old game and too polite, perhaps, for their own good—practically bursting with the quiet pride that is a trademark of the people of the Emerald City.

Thank goodness my father had married my mother, Vickie, a die-hard Dodgers fan. She used to listen to the games on the radio with her family when they were broadcast across the entire West Coast. In marrying my father, she kept the family tradition alive. Never give in; never admit defeat.

Without consulting any of my elders—indeed, without even realizing it until much later—I too, being the eldest son, defied my father's Yankees and chose the Giants of San Francisco. Please notice that I found a team that rebelled against both parents. Perhaps I got an extra strand of this mutinous family gene, because whoever the Yankees played—the Red Sox, the Tigers, even the Mariners—instantly became my favorite team du jour.

I prepared for days to break the news to my father, expecting a mighty quarrel. After all, contention and quarrelling were my motivation for choosing, right? When I made my announcement that not only was I a Yankee-hater of the highest order, but that my allegiances would forever lie with their sworn enemies, I think I might have seen his heart break ever so slightly in the momentary burden his eyes revealed. But he said nothing. I think he might even have cracked the tiniest of smiles. Perhaps he realized that the tradition, odd as it may be, had transpired in his nuclear family, just as it had in his own.

And thus, my younger brother, Sean, following his father, has stuck solidly by the Yankees all these years.

While I was in a Red Sox phase (they seemed to be the likeliest team to defeat the Yanks in '78), my brother flirted with switching his allegiances to please me. I was elated. I had pulled off something big here. I'd broken the cycle and managed a convert to my way of thinking. Plus, there would now be a majority against my father. It was a brilliant coup. Pure unplanned genius.

But sadly, his conversion lasted only a few days. Thinking back, I must have put a tad too much pressure on him when I forced him to memorize the starting lineups and batting averages of the Sox at the tender age of seven. We were sitting in my room and the quiz was to place the position players in their spots on a mock field I had drawn with my finger into the thick shag carpet. When he placed Carl Yastrzemski in center field, I went ballistic.

"No, no, no," I shrieked. "Yaz plays left. He took over the position from Ted Williams and has held it ever since. Fred Lynn is in center." This, however, wasn't completely true, as Yaz in '78 had been splitting his time in left with Jim Rice and DH-ing. But the point is, perhaps a more gentle elder brother might have been more patient with the little guy, but as I have said, I was a contentious youngster, firm in my understanding of right and wrong, good and evil.

When Sean announced his defiance of me—that he, in truth, loved the Yankees all along and hated the Red Sox (the little defector)—I knew that my filial rebellion had been crushed before it truly had begun and that this significant setback of my plan required immediate action. A donnybrook of epic proportions was in order.

So, with a #2 pencil I bored tiny holes into the mouths of all my Yankee baseball card player's pictures (the good ones; Reggie Jackson was sent to the gallows first), into which I shoved small, cigar-like firecrackers and then blew them off ceremoniously in a decidedly un-American twenty-one-bang salute. For the Yankee scrubs, I had reserved a special fate: clothes-pinning them against the spokes of the back tire of my bicycle. I found the motorcycle-like flapping sound they made very enjoyable and, as a bonus, after riding around for a while with, say, Ed Figueroa propelling me forward, I could determine that his inky face had been completely stripped off the bent and destroyed paper card, and that it was time for another Yankee to suffer the same fate. It was a little like checking the gas tank and properly maintaining my bike using the decaying fuel of Yankee bench players—it was extremely fulfilling for a twelve-year-old. Plus, the look on my brother's face was priceless.

He, of course, was too young for real Indian fireworks, and countered by forcing all his Red Sox cards to walk the plank and drown in the bathtub. They swelled up to five times their normal thickness, but that was about the extent of the damage. (The old Topps cards really held their color well, even underwater. I've never to this day found the equal of the '78 Topps baseball cards. They had that great baseball game that you could play on the backs of the cards.) Except that, baseball allegiances aside, he was reprimanded by both our parents for making an enormous mess.

Over the years, the entire O'Connell family has successfully been converted to Mariners fans—some, however, have been willing to dissolve allegiances with their former teams more reluctantly than others. My Grandpa, "Oke," the senior member of the Yankee contingent, finally swore them off for good after a few years of the Steinbrenner regime. He was a no-nonsense Yankee fan who grew tired of the Steinbrenner dog-and-pony show. And in Grandpa Oke I finally found my defector—the unlikeliest one of them all. We now all support and love the M's completely, although my father, brother, and an uncle or two will still root for the Yanks in the playoffs once the M's are out.

But during my childhood, things were much different. Even back then, I sensed in my father a strange sort of pride in my seditious choice of baseball teams. We've had great times over the years squabbling about whose team is better and whose team chokes in the playoffs. After all, it is a family tradition.

He [Steinbrenner] fires people like it's
a bodily function.
—George Costanza on the TV show *Seinfeld*

I will never have a heart attack. I give them.
—George Steinbrenner

Chapter Three

George Steinbrenner:
The Man, The Myth, The Felon

George Steinbrenner has a monstrous ego, a penchant for micro-managing his baseball team, and more cash than he could ever spend in his lifetime—but to watch him manage his baseball team, he certainly tries. We could write a whole book about all of the moronic things the self-proclaimed "Boss" has said and done through the years—be it calling his players out in the press, firing managers on whims, or just plain putting his foot in his mouth. But since we only have a few pages to devote to this walking caricature of megalomania, we thought we'd try to shed some light on who this guy is, where he came from, and how he became so powerful and demented.

George Martin Steinbrenner III was born on the Fourth of July in 1930. His father, Henry, had graduated at the top of his class at prestigious MIT, majoring in naval architecture. In addition to having a head for boat building, Henry also excelled in the low hurdles, winning a national collegiate championship in the 220-meter event in 1927. According to a May 10, 2004, *Sports Illustrated* article, Henry was a "stern disciplinarian" who dreamed that George would one day follow in his footsteps and attend MIT. After George distinguished himself at MIT—on the track and in the classroom—Henry supposed he would be ready to take over the family's Cleveland-based ship building business. No pressure on the Little Stein, right?

Henry's grand plan never materialized. There was one problem with little George. He was no whiz in the classroom. Apparently, George was the type of kid who spent more time picking his nose and cracking jokes that garnered no laughter than listening to his teachers. Even the rigorous boarding school he was forced to attend—Culver Military Academy—failed to whip him into shape. George was denied admission to MIT. So he attended Williams College instead, which is no slouch as a safety school. But the boy knew that he had let his old man down, and he never forgave himself. He vowed to become a Big Stein one day to show his father he was worthy of his respect. He would become a Stein who others admired and feared.

> When Georgie-Porgie talks, I don't listen.
> —then–Red Sox manager Jimy Williams

Eager to distinguish himself in the business world, George enrolled at Williams College as an English literature major—a savvy choice, no doubt. What faster path is there to success in this world than a degree in English literature? Just ask us. Josh is so successful that he's still driving the same car he was driving to his lit classes back in 1992. And Kevin is still wearing T-shirts that actually predate Josh's car.

Upon graduating from Williams in 1952, Steinbrenner joined the Air Force for a crash course in discipline. We figure it was his time in the service that taught him the value of close-cropped haircuts. In any case, Steinbrenner rose as high as second lieutenant before leaving the Air Force to take an assistant coaching position with the Northwestern University football team in 1955. The next season he moved to Purdue University, accepting a position in the same capacity. No wonder George plays the Grand Old Game with all of the finesse of a middle linebacker in heat.

After mastering the nuances of sports management in a few short years, Steinbrenner was ready to put Daddy's money to work. In 1961 he bought the Cleveland Pipers of the American Basketball League. The ABL was a fledgling circuit that hoped to rival the NBA. In the league's only full season, 1962, Steinbrenner's Pipers won the championship. But the campaign was not without controversy. Midway through the season, Pipers' head coach John McLendon quit, angered that Steinbrenner was constantly diagramming plays that he wanted the team to run. Steinbrenner hired Bill Sharman to finish the season. After the championship game, the league folded.

Ten years later, in 1972, Steinbrenner made a failed attempt to buy the Cleveland Indians. Oh, how things might be different in the world today if George had bought the Indians instead of the Yankees. But it was not to be. In January 1973, Steinbrenner led a group of investors that bought the New York Yankees for the meager sum of $10.3 million from CBS. Steinbrenner's personal equity stake in the enterprise amounted to just $168,000. These were happy days in the House of Stein, no doubt. But they didn't last long.

In 1974, Steinbrenner found himself in hot water when it was revealed by federal prosecutors that he was being investigated for his role in the Watergate scandal. Not only had he made illegal contributions to the president's reelection campaign, according to the government, but he had also lied to cover it up. On a hot August day, with famed Washington defense attorney Edward Bennett Williams by his side, Steinbrenner pled guilty in federal court to charges of making illegal campaign contributions to Richard Nixon and of obstructing justice. He was given a $15,000 fine, which amounted to a slap on the wrist. But baseball did not grant its brash new owner the same leniency the federal court system had. Commissioner Bowie Kuhn made a strong statement that there was no room in baseball for illegal, immoral characters when he handed Steinbrenner a two-year suspension from the game. The ban prevented the Yankee boss from attending major league games and from participating in the operations of his team. Accounts of George's activities during the suspension are sketchy at best, but we suspect he spent most of his time hatching

There is nothing as limiting as being a limited
partner with George Steinbrenner.
—John McMullen, one-time owner of the
Houston Astros and New Jersey Devils

plans for world domination or, at the very least, total domination of the baseball world.

> KEVIN: Maybe he sat around playing Risk all day.
> JOSH: It was the 1970s. Risk wasn't invented yet.
> KEVIN: Battleship then?
> JOSH: I bet Monopoly is his game.

One's a born liar, and the other's been convicted.
—Billy Martin, on Reggie Jackson and George Steinbrenner

Finally, on March 1, 1976, Kuhn commuted Steinbrenner's sentence, allowing him to return to the game after a sixteen-month hiatus. While columnist Red Smith continued to refer to the Yankee owner as "convicted felon George Steinbrenner" in the *New York Times*, Steinbrenner focused on improving his team, which had finished third in 1975. The Yankees welcomed back their owner by reaching the 1976 World Series. After being swept by the Reds in that October Classic, the Yankees bounced back to win the Series in 1977 and 1978.

Steinbrenner's emergence as one of baseball's most successful owners coincided with and was bolstered by the advent of free agency. After a series of legal decisions regarding baseball's antitrust exemption paved the way for a new collective bargaining agreement between the owners and players, the game's first free agent class hit the open market in the fall of 1976. The biggest star to change teams that off-season was Reggie Jackson, who signed with the Yankees. Steinbrenner flew to Chicago to close the deal himself. A few months later, Jackson arrived at the Yankees' spring training complex in Fort Lauderdale,

> Let [Steinbrenner]
> come in here and
> manage these guys and
> I'll spend the day
> counting his money.
> —Billy Martin

Florida, and George fawned over his new star like a little girl treats the new dolly she got for Christmas.

The Bronx Zoo was open for business, and did it ever make for some good tabloid fodder.

Jackson immediately made waves in the clubhouse by making such asinine comments as, "I didn't come to New York to be a star, I brought my star with me," and, "This team all flows from me. I've got to keep it all going. I'm the straw that stirs the drink. It all comes back to me. Maybe I should say me and [Thurman] Munson. But really—he doesn't enter into it."

Jackson's new teammates were irritated with his arrogance, while Yankee manager Billy Martin was threatened by Jackson's close relationship with Steinbrenner. The manager showed his disdain for Jackson by hitting him sixth or seventh in the batting order early in the 1977 season. As Yankee catcher Elston Howard reflected years later, "I think Billy wanted Jackson to fail more than he wanted the Yankees to win." Throughout the 1977 season Jackson and Martin took shots at each other in the dugout, clubhouse, and newspapers. They also made their feelings about one another known to Steinbrenner. But as long as the Yankees were winning—which they were—Steinbrenner didn't mind the acrimony. Rather, he seemed to thrive on it. Even early on in his tenure as Yankee boss, George displayed the rare ability to bring out the absolute worst in his fellow men and to take a strange kind of pleasure in doing so. It was true then, as it is today, that the closer someone became to George, the greater the likelihood that the person would become an egomaniacal bastard.

It's a good thing Babe Ruth isn't still with the Yankees. If he was, George Steinbrenner would have him bat seventh and say he's overweight.
—Graig Nettles

KEVIN: A deal with the devil and a contract with the Yankees. They're basically the same thing.
JOSH: Only God will always take you back. But once you're in Steinbrenner's clutches, you're a lost soul.

As far as we can tell, George's main problem has always been that he has a very warped sense of values. To him, so long as a player is clean-shaven, sports a crew cut, and looks good in pinstripes, the player is a professional. In the 1980s, Steinbrenner made the team's most popular and arguably most classy player the object of his ire when he engaged in a protracted public spat with Don Mattingly over whether or not the first baseman would shave his mustache and trim his bangs. And some things never change. On the first day of Spring Training 2005, Randy Johnson showed up at Yankees' camp sans his trademark mullet, courtesy of the Boss's metaphoric shears.

In the building I live in on Park Avenue there are ten people who could buy the Yankees, but none of them could hit the ball out of Yankee Stadium.
—Reggie Jackson

JOSH: Clearly, the man hates hair.
KEVIN: Have you ever seen Stein without a shirt on?
JOSH: No. Can't say that I want to either.
KEVIN: Me neither. But I bet he shaves his body hair.

In any case, midway through the 1978 season as both Jackson and Steinbrenner questioned his every move, Martin resigned. Steinbrenner rehired Martin and subsequently fired him four times in the next ten years. According to rumors, at the time of Martin's drunk driving death in 1989, Steinbrenner was contemplating bringing him back for a sixth tour of duty in the Big Apple.

The 1980s represented one of the least successful decades in Yankee history. The team changed managers twelve times during the decade, while shuffling scores of players in and out of New York via trades and the free-agent market. Steinbrenner made abusive phone calls to his managers in the middle of games when they made decisions he didn't like. And he often questioned the integrity of his players in the New York tabloids. George was out of control, and eventually it caught up with him. Amidst a public dispute with Yankee slugger Dave Winfield, Steinbrenner paid $40,000 to Howard Spira, a renowned gambler from the Bronx, to fabricate incriminating evidence against Winfield. In 1990, Commissioner Fay Vincent handed Steinbrenner a lifetime ban from baseball. When it was announced during a game at Yankee Stadium that Steinbrenner's involvement with the team was essentially finished, the fans in attendance responded with a ninety-second standing ovation. But in 1993 Vincent inexplicably allowed Steinbrenner to resume his previous post at the Yankees helm.

> Joe Torre doesn't ask me for help anymore, so I don't give it to him. I don't call down to the dugout anymore.
> —George Steinbrenner

Talk about second and third chances . . . and we thought MLB's drug policy was lax (insert your own Steve Howe joke here).

Following the previous pattern, soon after Steinbrenner returned from his suspension, the team began another string of championship seasons, and before long New York fans were treating George like a king once again. Perhaps having learned from his mistakes, Steinbrenner stayed under the radar during the Yankees' championship seasons in the mid- to late-1990s. And he stuck with one manager: Joe Torre.

> George will have full control as long as he's breathing. —Lou Piniella

New Yorkers would be foolish though to think George has truly changed. There have been increasing signs that he is meddling again. And when George meddles, calamity usually ensues. For example, the Yankees' failure to retain star pitcher Andy Pettitte—lost to Houston as a free agent prior to the 2004 season—was reportedly the result of Steinbrenner's concerns regarding the lefty's toughness. And sources close to the team suggested that the acquisitions of gifted but selfish players like Raul Mondesi, Kenny Lofton, and Gary Sheffield were the result of Steinbrenner pressuring general manager Brian Cashman to make these deals. Now, we're not saying a player like Sheffield isn't a darned good player. What we're saying is that he's not the type of unselfish player who cares only about winning that led the Torre Yankees to their championships in the 1990s. Sheffield might have produced big numbers on the field for the Yanks in his first season with the team, but he also created more than his fair share of distractions. First, a *Sports Illustrated* article brought to light a public dispute between Sheffield and Barry Bonds when the former claimed the latter stole his personal chef out from under him with a more lucrative salary offer. Then, Sheffield spouted inflammatory comments about the Red Sox after Game 3 of the 2004 ALCS, contributing Boston bulletin board material to the Red Sox rallying cry. Then, he admitted to using performance-enhancing drugs, claiming that he did so unknowingly. Then, he walked out on the Yankees briefly during Spring Training 2005 in a dispute over whether or not he would be paid interest on the deferred portion of his 2004 salary.

In short, he brought a lot of baggage with him to New York and a level of selfishness that could only detract from team chemistry.

Torre's World Series winning clubs were characterized by gritty players like Paul O'Neil, Scott Brosius, and Joe Girardi who didn't fit the "Me-first" mold that characterized the Bronx Zoo Yankees of the 1970s and 1980s. Torre's Yankees played well together and often put the good of the team before their own egos. Recent incarnations of the team, however, suggest that Steinbrenner's misguided values are weighing increasingly heavily in personnel decisions once again. For Yankee fans, that's not a good sign. For barbershops in the Bronx and for the rest of us, that's just fine. We'll happily sit back and watch the whole dysfunctional Yankee Empire implode, despite its astronomical resources. Hey, we can dream, can't we?

Working for George Steinbrenner was like doing two tours in Vietnam and not getting killed. It was the craziest two and a half years of my life . . . Basically, it didn't matter what I did, George Steinbrenner was going to kick my ass. If I walked into his office with a briefcase full of a million dollars, he would have yelled at me that they weren't $100 bills, that they were twenties. So first you have to know that it doesn't matter what you do, he's going to kick your ass.

—Joe Perello, former Yankees vice president of business development, as quoted in *Sports Illustrated*

Chapter Four

Trader Josh

Josh here, remembering a defining moment in my childhood.

Growing up, I would look forward to the summers when my cousins, Mike and Kim Coney, would travel from Patterson, New Jersey, to my family's house in rural Massachusetts to spend a week with our family. Mike and Kim were city kids who really enjoyed doing all those country things my brother and I took for granted, like building forts in the woods, fishing, and camping out in the backyard. Additionally, Mike and I had a shared passion for baseball card collecting. Mike was a Yankee fan, but this actually worked out well because we both loved to trade cards. I would save a year's worth of Yankee cards, and he would save a year's worth of Red Sox cards, and then each summer we would orchestrate a series of trades to purge our collections of enemy forces. He would pretend to be George Steinbrenner, saying obnoxious things and making inane comments, while I would pretend to be Red Sox general manager Lou Gorman, hemming and hawing theatrically before pulling the trigger on each deal—which usually favored the Yankees.

I remember acquiring a Marty Barrett rookie card in exchange for a Don Mattingly rookie and thinking that I'd just pulled off the trade of the century. To this day I have a closet full of boxes that contain cards of Steve Crawford, Mark Clear, Jerry Remy, Rick Miller, Dave Stapleton, Glen Hoffman, Ed Jurak, and other Boston scrubs that I received from my cousin in exchange for cards of Mattingly, Dave Winfield, Rickey Henderson, Dave Righetti, Ron Guidry, and other Yankee stars.

The Yankees of the early 1980s had much better players than the Red Sox teams of the era, and, as a result, I was acquiring "commons" (as worthless baseball cards are known) in exchange for cards that were actually worth something. Of course, I didn't know this at the time, and my cousin didn't either. We were trading based purely on team loyalty and our love of collecting.

In the mid-1980s when the baseball card business really boomed and card price guides started appearing on drugstore magazine racks, Mike and I realized just how lopsided some of our past trades had been. The Don Mattingly rookie card, for example, was listed at $240, while the Marty Barrett rookie card was listed at four cents. Clearly, the Yankee Bias extended even to the world of baseball card collecting.

When our respective mothers caught wind of how Mike had inadvertently swindled me, Mike, to his credit, offered to undo some of our previous deals. Through another series of lopsided trades, he would return to me the valuable Yankee cards he had acquired for valueless Red Sox cards. I was tempted to take him up on his generous offer. I thought about reacquiring that Don Mattingly card and making it the centerpiece of my collection. I also thought about taking it back and then selling it. The deal came very close to happening. It was to the point where I was actually holding the Barrett in my left hand and the Mattingly in my right as I sat across from my cousin at the kitchen table. On their respective cards, Barrett was making a sidearm throw from second base, while Mattingly was posed, staring wistfully into the camera.

"Of course you'll make the deal," my cousin hissed in his best faux-Steinbrenner. "It all comes down to money. Cash is king."

Perhaps this was the closest I ever came to being lured over to the Dark Side of baseball's greatest rivalry. For just a moment, I was tempted to sell out Marty Barrett for Donny Baseball. Hey, $240 sounds like a hell of a lot to a twelve-year-old kid who's rolling pennies and collecting soda cans to support a $20-per-week Donruss and Topps habit.

Thankfully, in the end I did the right thing. I carefully put Marty Barrett back in his protective plastic sleeve—as if he needed one—and then returned him to his place of honor in my box where he belonged. Then I put Don Mattingly back in his sleeve and pushed him across the table to my cousin, as if the card was riddled with scurvy. In my best Lou Gorman voice I said, "Mattingly? Another first baseman? Where would we play him? We've already got Buckner."

39

Oh, how cruel the ironies of being a Red Sox fan can be.

In any case, the baseball card bubble has since burst, and now the Mattingly card, like the Barrett card, can be bought at any card store for pocket change, which is probably the way things should have been all along. Baseball cards are for kids (and for the kid in all of us), not for junior stockbrokers and professional "collectors." But I still wake up in a cold sweat every so often, having just made the trade and at the same time having handed over my integrity. But then I realize that it was just a dream. While it is true that many of my diamond heroes—Wade Boggs, Roger Clemens, and company— have turned to the Dark Side, I know that I never will.

Chapter Five

Over-Played, Over-Hyped, Overrated

The volume of national media treatment that the Yankees receive and the content of that treatment both contribute to the widespread belief that the Yankees are an extra-special team, composed of especially gifted players. While we can't deny that the Yankees do usually have a more talented roster than other teams, we believe a case can be made that many of New York's players are overrated by fans across the country due to the additional exposure their association with the Yankees brings them.

To start, let's consider the considerable airtime the Yankees receive throughout the regular season on national TV at the expense of other equally deserving teams and how this affects the game's fan base. If we accept that fans are more apt to root for teams and players who they feel they know better, clearly the Yankees have an advantage over other teams when it comes to building a fan base outside of their primary market. Everyone knows that Derek Jeter plays shortstop for the New York Yankees because, no matter where a person lives, he sees the Yankees on TV all the time. But let's face it, how many people outside of Kansas City can name the current shortstop of the Kansas City Royals? Thus, Derek Jeter's fans span from sea to shining sea, while there are far fewer Angel Berroa fans out there, or whoever's covering short for KC these days.

Not only do the Yankees receive preferential treatment from the networks in the form of plentiful national broadcasts, but the coverage they receive usually reflects a decidedly pro-Yankee slant. In other words, broadcasters from FOX, ESPN, C-SPAN, and even Animal Planet love to sing the Yankees' laurels, referring time and time again to the same tired clichés. Fans are told the Yankees are classy and that the pinstripes have a way of making great players out of good players, so they believe these glorifications and summarily pile onto the pinstriped happy wagon without stopping to actually form an opinion of their own.

In a perfect world, kids in Pigs Knuckles, Arkansas, Topeka, Kansas, and Sulfur, Louisiana, would have equal access to all teams and players and would decide for themselves which ones they liked best. But this is not a perfect world. This is a world in which the dollar apparently rules supreme, and the Yankees are a proven commodity in the ratings game. The big advertising agencies, most of which are located on Madison Avenue in New York, want to put their clients' bucks behind a winner. They don't want to pitch deodorant and erectile enhancement pills between innings of an Oakland A's and Chicago White Sox game. That's just not sexy. They want to be associated with winning teams and winning players. So the FOX Game of the Week perpetually pits the Pinstripes against whichever patsy New York happens to be pummeling that Saturday. Inevitably, the kids who don't have a hometown team of their own, or who have a perennial non-contender in their own backyard, start to root for the Yankees. They ask Mom and Dad to buy them Yankee hats and Yankee jackets, and eventually when they're old enough they sign up for their own Yankee credit cards so they can buy Derek Jeter bobble-head dolls over the Internet and books like *Yankee Century* from the YES network. And with every purchase they make, the Yankee Empire grows richer and more powerful, leaping and bounding ahead of all other teams in the revenue department.

> **JOSH:** The Yanks make consistent merchandise bucks year in and year out, while other teams are left to hope and pray that some street gang will adopt their colors and start scarfing up hats and jerseys.
> **KEVIN:** Yeah, I heard the Bloods are wearing Cincinnati red this year.

Sadly, this media effect is nothing new. It was going on in the days of black-and-white TV when Home Run Derby aired, trotting out one Yankee slugger after another, and it was going on in the 1980s when ABC introduced Monday Night Baseball, which could have been more aptly titled The Yankee Game of the Week.

All the while, the media justifies the extra airtime it gives the Yankees by simply stating that fans want to see the best baseball out there, and the Yankees are the best team. When questions related to George Steinbrenner's business practices arise, journalists are quick to remind fans that the Yankees are playing by the rules: There is no salary cap in baseball, and the Yankees are free to spend as much money as they'd like. They tell Yankee detractors that if Steinbrenner owned their team, they'd love him for spending so lavishly on players, and in doing so they completely discount the dozens of unseemly incidents involving Steinbrenner that have embarrassed the

Yankees and baseball since he joined the game. Then these same individuals offer the flawed logic that the money the Yankees spend doesn't really matter anyway. "Look at the Twins," they say. "They have a low payroll but continue to make the playoffs. That proves money doesn't guarantee a title." This is precisely where the Yankee defenders cross the line into sheer lunacy. Yes, the Twins have won a few division titles in the league's weakest division, but they've also bowed out of the postseason tournament early every time without reaching the World Series. Their payroll does not allow them much chance to compete on a level playing field against the other playoff teams. Consider the 2004 American League Division Series between the Twins and the Yankees. Minnesota had Justin Morneau, a mid-season call-up, hitting cleanup, while New York had Alex Rodriguez, who would bat cleanup on any other team, hitting in the two-hole. More than that, the Twins sent a mediocre pitcher like Carlos Silva to the mound to start the crucial third game, while the Yankees had the luxury of holding back Javier Vazquez (who would be the ace on many teams) until the fourth game. When Vazquez struggled in Game 4, the Yankees handed the ball over to Esteban Loaiza, a twenty-game winner the year before, who had yet to pitch in the Series. To no one's surprise, the Yankees were just too deep for the Twins to overcome, just as they'd been too deep for the over-achieving money-ball A's in previous years.

The All-Star Game offers another forum for the media to hype the Yankees and propagate the belief among fans that certain Yankees players are better than they actually are. In recent years, it seems like every Mid-Summer Classic includes at least one or two Yankees who don't have superior statistics but make the AL team to the exclusion of more deserving players on other teams. That is because the fans pick the starting position players for the game, and the manager of the defending league champion (often the Yankees' manager in recent years) picks the reserves and pitchers. Fans attending ballparks across the nation are more apt to punch the chads of players who have household names than players whose names they barely know.

> **KEVIN:** Let's see, Victor Martinez or Jorge Posada. At
> least I've heard of Posada.
> **JOSH:** Martinez was on your fantasy team last year,
> dimwit.
> **KEVIN:** Some fantasy, eh?

Hence, in 2004 fans voted Derek Jeter and Jason Giambi to start the All-Star Game, even though Jeter was off to the worst start of his career and Giambi had missed much of the season's first half with health complications that we would later learn were steroid related. So, Jeter and Giambi were on the team, along with six other Yankees, giving New York one-quarter of the spots on the thirty-two-man squad—and if not for the rule that every team must be represented by at least one player, there would have certainly been even more Yankees on the team. As it was, the fan vote resulted in an infield of Yankee Jason Giambi at first base, former Yankee Alfonso Soriano (who had just been traded to the Rangers) at second, Yankee Derek Jeter at short, and Yankee Alex Rodriguez at third. For good measure, former Yankee Roger Clemens started the game for the NL. Just in case things got hairy in the late innings, AL manager Joe Torre had added Yankees Hideki Matsui and Gary Sheffield to his bench and Mariano Rivera, Tom Gordon, and Javier Vazquez to his bullpen. The suspect selection of Gordon, a set-up-man, continued a long tradition of Torre selecting Yankees' middle-relievers, with Mike Stanton and Jeff Nelson as previous examples. Meanwhile, Vazquez—who New York couldn't unload quick enough after a dismal second half—made the team instead of eventual AL Cy Young Award winner Johan Santana.

When casual fans and youngsters across the country tune-in to the Mid-Summer Classic and see an AL squad composed of 25 percent Yankees, many assume that the Yankees *really are* that good. They assume that Tom Gordon must be one of the league's twelve best pitchers. Hard-core baseball fans know better, but the average fan does not. And so the snowball effect continues. Fans believe Yankee players are better than they actually are. The networks and advertising agencies keep hyping them, and the players' images continue to rise in the realm of public opinion.

But the commissioner's office isn't going to complain if the Yankees make up a quarter of the AL squad, because that's exactly what FOX wants. If the TV fat cats are happy, Uncle Bud is happy. Giambi, Jeter, and Torre are the ones hawking the underwear and credit cards, so the more "face time" they get, the better.

KEVIN: When did it stop being about baseball and start being about advertising?
JOSH: Welcome to the Dark Side, young Skywalker.

Later in the year, baseball's postseason again provides the Yankees with an opportunity to gain new fans nationwide. Throughout the playoffs, which the Yankees make every year, the national broadcasters continually remind viewers that the Yankees always "rise to the occasion in the postseason," and that Yankee teams are "built to perform in the clutch." The Yankees, we are told, have history, aura, mystique, and seemingly every other intangible on their side. Whenever New York falters in a postseason game or series, our friendly national announcers reassure us that "it will be okay; the team's mystique will take over, and the team will bounce back." It's as if they assume most viewers are rooting for the Pinstripes. Okay, so maybe the buffet table in the Yankee Stadium media room serves filet mignon; if they want to root for the Yanks, that's their business, but they shouldn't force that mind-set on the rest of the nation. The reporting is almost as biased as FOX News.

The 2003 ALCS between the Yankees and Red Sox demonstrated how far the networks stray from providing unbiased coverage. For all seven games of the Series, Mariners third baseman Brett Boone provided play-by-play "analysis" in the FOX broadcast booth. Such player cameos are ordinarily useless enough in their own right, but this time the situation was even worse. Talk about a Yankee Bias: Boone's younger brother, Aaron, was playing third base for the Yankees all series long. It wasn't tough to figure out which team Big Brother was rooting for. Is it too much to ask that the broadcasters selected to call the biggest games of the year be completely unbiased and neutral? We don't blame Brett Boone—of course he's going to root for his brother's team. We blame the network for putting someone with an obvious rooting interest in the booth instead of a completely objective journalist—of course, finding one on staff at FOX might have proved a bit difficult.

The members of the cheering baseball press, however, have historically favored the Yankees above all other teams. This favoritism is often reflected in the annual Baseball Writers Association of America Awards, which are announced at the end of each season (MVP, Cy Young Award, Rookie of the Year). And this leads to another way in which the national media contributes to how the game's players are perceived and how its history books are written.

Below are the facts and stats related to just a few of the controversial votes by the Baseball Writers Association through the years. Now, we know that defenders of the Yankees and of the press will say that the first two cases involving Ted Williams occurred because the press hated Williams and loved good-old-boys like Joe DiMaggio and the other Yankees of the era who would sip whiskey and play cards with the scribes. We say this type of logic only serves to further underscore the problem of media bias.

CASE 1: THE 1942 AL MVP AWARD

Ted Williams led the AL in six major offensive categories. But Yankee Joe Gordon, who led the league in zero offensive categories, won the MVP award. Perhaps the writers concluded that Gordon brought more "intangibles" to the table?

1942 AL Batting Statistics

	G	R	H	HR	RBI	BA	OBP	SLG
Gordon	147	88	173	18	103	.322	.409	.491
Williams	150	**141**	186	**36**	**137**	**.356**	**.499**	**.648**

* Bold type indicates the player led the league in this category.

CASE 2: THE 1947 AL MVP AWARD

Despite another remarkable season by Williams—one in which he again led the AL in six major offensive categories—it was more of the same when it came time for the sportswriters to select the MVP. Williams finished second in the balloting to DiMaggio, despite superior statistics in every single major offensive category.

1947 AL Batting Statistics

	G	R	H	HR	RBI	BA	OBP	SLG
DiMaggio	141	97	168	20	97	.315	.391	.522
Williams	156	**125**	181	**32**	**114**	**.343**	**.499**	**.634**

* Bold type indicates the player led the league in this category.

Where have you gone, Joe DiMaggio? A nation turns its lonely eyes to you.

—Paul Simon, "Mrs. Robinson"

"Have faith in the Yankees, my son," the old man told the boy. "Think of the great DiMaggio."

—Ernest Hemingway, *The Old Man and the Sea*

CASE 3: THE 1960 WORLD SERIES MVP AWARD

The awards handed out in the postseason are also decided by the writers and are subject to this same pro–Yankee Bias. One of the most glaring examples of the writers' favoritism occurred in 1960 when Pirates second baseman Bill Mazeroski hit a walk-off home run in the bottom of the ninth inning in Game 7 of the World Series and then, after circling the bases, watched the Yankees' Bobby Richardson collect the MVP trophy. Did the writers fail to notice that the Pirates had won the World Series? Did they notice that Mazeroski drove in the winning run in three of the Pirates' four Series wins? Sure, Richardson (.367 series average) had three more hits (eleven to eight) than Mazeroski (.320) in the series, but Mazeroski got the hits that mattered most and the Pirates were the Series winner.

CASE 4: THE 1999 AL MVP AWARD

Even in the present day, the media favors Yankee players. In 1999, for example, Red Sox pitcher Pedro Martinez lost his bid for the AL MVP Award despite receiving more first place votes than any other player in the league. Martinez finished second because *New York Post* writer George King left him entirely off his ballot. That means that

King did not consider Martinez—who had won the pitching Triple Crown—one of the top ten players in the AL. King gave his top vote to Jeter, who finished sixth overall in the balloting with . . . one first place vote. (P.S. We find it more than just coincidental that this writer's name when reversed is King George.)

What do all of these trends add up to? Overrated Yankee players being over-represented in the baseball history books. While it is undeniable that the Yankees have had many superb players over the years, the facts remain that nearly every Yankee rookie is labeled the next big star (Kevin Maas, Roberto Kelly, Ricky Ledee, Drew Henson, Shane Spencer, Hensley "Bam Bam" Meulens), the team's good players are prematurely deified (Don Mattingly, Bernie Williams, Dave Righetti), and many of the Yankees' supposed diamond kings (Phil Rizzuto, Reggie Jackson, Thurman Munson) were, in reality, very good players but not members of baseball's most elite class of all-time greats. Rather than launching into a full-fledged attack on all thirty-nine Yankees in the Hall of Fame, we will examine the cases of two—Rizzuto and Jackson—to illuminate our point.

First off: Rizzuto. We could make this a very short discussion by discounting all of his accomplishments on the field due to his horrendous broadcasting career in the years that followed his playing career, but we believe the two should be separate. Before becoming the "Holy Cow" homer, the "Scooter" played thirteen seasons with the Yankees and won ten AL Pennants. Boy, was he ever in the right place at the right time. If he had played for the White Sox, he would be remembered as his generation's Ozzie Guillen, a light-hitting shortstop who played well in the field and didn't hurt his team too much at the plate. But because Rizzuto wore pinstripes, he is enshrined in the Hall of Fame. Below we offer Rizzuto's stats compared to an assortment of mediocre shortstops, none of whom are in the Hall of Fame. Mind you, this is NOT a list of other shortstops who we believe should be en-shrined in Cooperstown. Rather it is a list of average shortstops from other teams who, like Rizzuto, clearly do not belong in the Hall.

	G	R	H	2B	HR	RBI	AVG	OBP	SLG
Phil Rizzuto	1661	877	1588	239	38	563	.273	.351	.355
Gary Templeton	2079	893	2096	329	70	728	.271	.306	.369
Tony Fernandez	2158	1057	2276	414	94	844	.288	.347	.399
Dick Bartell	2016	1130	2165	442	79	710	.284	.351	.391
Rick Burleson	1346	656	1401	256	50	449	.273	.331	.361
Dave Concepcion	2488	993	2326	389	101	950	.267	.322	.357

Note that all of the players on this list collected more hits than games played except for Rizzuto and Concepcion. When it came time for the Veterans Committee to judge him, though, the Scooter had one thing going for him that all of the other players didn't: He was a lifetime Yankee and had basked in the warm glow of media spotlight that being a well-liked Yankee offers.

> I heard doctors revived a man who had been dead for four and a half minutes. When they asked him what it was like being dead, he said it was like listening to Yankees announcer Phil Rizzuto during a rain delay.
>
> —David Letterman

The case of Reggie Jackson provides an example of how a very good player can be elevated to legendary status due to his association with the Yankees. We are not arguing that Jackson does not belong in the Hall of Fame or that he was not a clutch player. We simply argue that he does not deserve the near universal recognition he seems to receive as one of the game's all-time elite players. He was a one-dimensional player who did one thing well: He hit home runs (a lot of them). For that he deserves his place in Cooperstown. He also struck out more times than any other player in the history of the game and batted just .262 in his career. Jackson's name should never be mentioned in the same breath as multidimensional sluggers like Ted Williams, Stan Musial, Joe DiMaggio, and Hank Aaron. However, it often is, both by Jackson himself and by the swarming hordes of pro-Yankee media members and the mindless goons who follow them. The table below compares Jackson's home run ratio and strikeout ratio to other sluggers who are not normally considered anything more than just that—sluggers who didn't bring much more to the game than their power strokes.

	AB	HR	HR/AB	K	K/AB
Reggie Jackson	9864	563	1/17.5	2597	1/3.8
Cecil Fielder	5157	319	1/16.1	1316	1/3.9
Jose Canseco	7057	462	1/15.2	1942	1/3.6
Dave Kingman	6677	442	1/15.1	1816	1/3.7
Darryl Evans	8973	414	1/21.7	1410	1/6.3
Gorman Thomas	4677	268	1/17.5	1339	1/3.5

As you can see, Jackson homered less often and struck out more often than many of these players. Yet, only Jackson, among this group, is enshrined in the Hall of Fame, and only Jackson is considered one of the game's great players. This is due both to the longevity of his career and to the fact that he will forever be associated with the Yankees. Oh, and we suppose there is the matter of the three home runs he hit in one World Series game. We seem to remember Adam Kennedy hitting three home runs in a playoff game for the Angels in 2002, but we don't suppose we'll see a plaque for him in Cooperstown any time soon.

> **JOSH:** That Reggie Bar made me awfully sick.
> **KEVIN:** That was from 1979. You weren't supposed to eat it. You were supposed to study it, and make it part of the discussion.
> **JOSH:** Oops.

I am the best in baseball.

—**Reggie Jackson**

The only reason I don't like playing in the World Series is I can't watch myself play.

—**Reggie Jackson**

[Reggie Jackson] would give you the shirt off his back. Of course he'd call a press conference to announce it.

—**Catfish Hunter**

The bottom line is that the Yankees take care of the media by providing plenty of advertising dollars, and the media takes care of the Yankees by building them up to be more prolific than they actually are. So, the myth that the Yankees possess a special mystique is perpetuated and the dollars keep pouring into the Yankees' coffers.

Chapter Six

Film Review: *Damn Yankees*

When we sat down to hash out this book, we wanted to enlist the help of all the anti-Yankee voices we could find. After all, since the Yankees have been the bullies on the block for as long as anyone can remember, surely there must be dozens of pop culture references dedicated to the cause of telling the truth about the Bronx Bummers. Or so we thought. We had no such luck. Other than the *Seinfeld* episodes that portrayed Steinbrenner as a blathering buffoon, it seemed that every other time the Yanks were mentioned in the universe of popular culture, it was with praise (of all things). And even that *Seinfeld* characterization of the Big Stein made him out to be more of an incompetent—almost a well-intentioned and fading senile old grandfatherly figure—than what he really is: "a bad man, Jerry, a very bad man." How else could George Costanza get a promotion after doing donuts in the Yankee Stadium parking lot with one of the Yankees' many World Series trophies dragging on the pavement behind his car, all the while berating Stein's ludicrous behavior over a megaphone for all to hear? This is sadly not the Steinbrenner that we all love to hate.

We quickly became frustrated in our search. It seemed that every piece of pop culture we could unearth echoed the media hype about the Yanks. One notable exception is the *Bad News Bears*—perhaps the greatest baseball movie of all time—in which the evil, bullying champions of the league don the pinstripes and the proud name of Yankees. What a classic. However, we thirsted for more.

Then, as luck would have it, we came across the baseball musical movie entitled *Damn Yankees*, and it occurred to us that there was also a "hair band" of the same name that was big in the early 1990s. The group paired the talents of the bow-hunting Ted Nugent's ten digits of doom and Tommy Shaw of Styx fame. Since our last chance at finding some anti-Yankee pop culture came down to watching a movie (formerly a lavish Broadway Musical) and listening to the collected works of possibly the most pathetic attempt at a Super Group in the history of rock music, we naturally went with the Super Group. Trouble was, and we say this with a considerable amount of certitude, the band had not written a single lyric that had anything to do with Yankee baseball. We were pretty sure the line "Can you take me high enough?" wasn't talking about a metaphorical baseball high of a Yankee-free universe. So, we reluctantly sat down to watch the movie.

> **JOSH:** I don't know if I can sit through a whole movie with people breaking into song and dance for no reason whatsoever. It makes my skin crawl. It just seems so pointless.
> **KEVIN:** Kind of like a Yankee win?

JOSH: Exactly.

KEVIN: What if watching this movie helps us prove how evil the Yankees are?

JOSH: For that, I would storm the gates of hell.

KEVIN: That's the spirit.

The film tells the story of Joe, an old and broken-down Washington Senators' fan, who out of desperation sells his soul to the Devil (played by Ray Walston—you know, Mr. Hand, from *Fast Times at Ridgemont High*). In exchange for his soul, Joe is permitted to become young again, to be the greatest ballplayer of all time, and most importantly, to beat them Damn Yankees. When Joe confronts the Devil to offer an escape clause in the contract for his soul, the Devil says: "I would do it, but I don't want to have those Damn Yankees win." Joe counters, "You can say that again."

JOSH: Hey, this movie has some promise.

KEVIN: Wait until the singing starts.

We watched on with renewed hope. We were very encouraged during another scene dealing with how teams tend to choke when playing New York. Certainly this scene was going to provide us with our much sought after myth-shattering logic. The matter was brought up in the Senators' locker room before a big game against the Yanks:

ROCKY: "It's just that when we play the Yankees, I kinda tense up. I lose my head. I figure what the heck's the use?"

MANAGER BENNY (TO SMOKEY): "Are you listening to this?"

SMOKEY: "Benny, there *is* something different about them."

BENNY: "What do you mean?"

ROCKY: "Well, we don't make the same goofs when we're playing Kansas City."

We were incredulous after this scene. Was there no end to this sucking up to the grandeur and mystique and aura of the Yankees? Another scene that gave us fits was when Benny was talking to a reporter and thinking of giving Joe a tryout.

BENNY: "Why make something out of the Yankees? They're a swell bunch of fellas."

REPORTER: "Oh yes, they're very polite . . . then they beat your brains out."

BENNY: "They're just another ball club."

DEVIL (DISGUISED AS JOE'S SCOUT): "I read somewhere they're thinking of handicapping the Yankees . . . making them wear extra weight, like racehorses."

After this scene, Kevin nearly chucked the DVD player out the window. But Josh protested. He reasoned that the Devil was merely (and falsely) trying to build up the threat of the Yankees so that Joe could get a tryout. "He was lying," Josh said, "and he's bashing false Yankee hype."

"I suppose," Kevin said. "But if there's any more Yankee butt-smooching in this movie, I'm sending it back."

We watched on—Kevin skeptically and Josh more optimistically. It was a reversal of roles for us, but the Damn Yankees can turn the world upside down. Right appears to be wrong, and wrong, right.

Then things took a turn for the better. Joe gets his shot at stardom, and he turns out to be just what the ball club needs. He crushes the ball at the plate, fields like Willie Mays, and has a cannon for an arm in center field. And most importantly, the Senators begin to whoop the Yanks game after game and capture the AL lead.

> **KEVIN:** Now this is a story I can get behind.
> **JOSH:** You see? You just need to be more patient.

The film's climactic scene comes when Joe is accused of taking a bribe, years earlier down in the Mexican League.

> **ROCKY:** "Joe ain't done nothing wrong. I'll bet you the Yankees are behind this whole thing."
> **ANOTHER SENATOR:** "Yeah, they're scared of us."

Of course Joe is exonerated but, in the movie's twist of fate, is simultaneously tricked into forgoing his escape clause. Although his soul is damned to eternal hell and he's obviously pretty down about it, the good news is that he gets to play in the game that will win the pennant and at long last vanquish his mortal enemies, the Yankees. So we're to assume that it's worth it.

> **KEVIN:** Such a heartwarming story.
> **JOSH:** Remember, it's worth it . . . damnation to eternal hell is worth it.

In the final game, Mickey Mantle makes the last out. He hits a shot to center field that Joe moves toward to end the game. But before our hero Joe makes the grab, the Devil reneges on his end of the bargain and changes young Joe back to old Joe. Old Joe still makes the catch and disappears out the door in the center field wall of Griffith Stadium, never to be heard from again. The Senators win the pennant, and Joe gets his soul back. And to top it all off, there is much speculation that New York gamblers have caused foul play with Joe's disappearance, further besmudging the Yankees' reputation.

> **KEVIN:** I love happy endings.
> **JOSH:** I'm not crying . . . I must've got some dust in my eye from this DVD.

Now you might be wondering what moral we can extract from this movie? First and foremost, the lesson is that there are more important things in life (and baseball) than merely winning: like beating the Yankees while keeping your soul intact, for example. Don't go becoming just as bad as the Yankees in order to beat them. (Are you listening Red Sox Nation?)

Second, in his attempts to thwart Joe, in the end the Devil transforms young Joe back to his normal old broken-down self, hoping that old Joe won't make the play. But old Joe musters up the stuff to make the final grab to defeat the Yankees, much to the Devil's chagrin. And because the Devil changed him back earlier than promised, the contract for his soul is voided. We interpret this to mean that we all have our part to play, young and old, sick and infirm in Yankee destruction. No act against the Evil Empire, no matter how small or insignificant, will go unrewarded in the end.

Finally, and perhaps most important, we must learn from this movie that George Steinbrenner is the modern manifestation of Ray Walston's Devil character. Just look at the similarities. Stein tries to rule over the lives and contracts of players, manipulating whenever he can (remember Dave Winfield), and generally attempts to wreak as much havoc with others as possible. And for what? All to fill his roster with the best "souls" that he can find—in an unholy quest of winning at any cost. Does the Devil play fair? No, and neither does Steinbrenner—and even though they are both technically following the established rules of their all too similar contract games, it's the rules of the game that turn out to be just as evil as those who make a mockery of them.

Okay, if Stein is not Lucifer himself, he is certainly one of the Devil's more powerful minions, or at least one of Ray Walston's more powerful minions.

But perhaps the most important point of all is that while all the other characterizations of Steinbrenner and the Yankees in the media are hopelessly filled with the stock Yankee adoration, the film *Damn Yankees* does well to portray the Bronx Bombers as they are: devilishly plotting your destruction.

JOSH: And I even enjoyed the dancing.
KEVIN: Well, Bob Fosse did the choreography.
JOSH: I wonder if he's related to Ray Fosse?

I wasn't trying to turn around the outcome of the game. I was just trying to get a ball. I'm starting to understand what it did. It struck me this morning when I woke up. Wow! I may have really helped the Yankees win.

—Jeffrey Maier, a twelve-year-old fan who caught a fair ball hit by Derek Jeter in a Yankee ALDS victory against the Orioles in 1996. The "home run" tied the game at 4–4 in the eighth. The Yankees won 5–4 in eleven innings.

Chapter Seven

Yankee Fans— Just What Makes 'em Tick?

Let us turn our attention now to the rather hefty fan base that the Yankees enjoy. While it seems easy to look at the many negative effects on the game that Yankee fans have enacted over the years, and to humiliate them personally by pointing out their many faults or engaging in name calling, we will not stoop to such lowly tactics. Rather, we have learned in our quest to understand all that is wrong with the baseball world to "love the sinner, hate the sin," so to speak. We feel no obligation to rehabilitate these misguided fans. Rather, we feel that a study of Yankee fans will prove fruitful in providing the entire baseball world with a better understanding of just what exactly is wrong with the game at its very heart and core. These so-called *most* *loyal fans in the game* are one of the primary reasons we decided to write the book. Call their bad behavior inspirational.

So this chapter will be dedicated to learning just what in the world these fans could possibly be thinking. We will reserve judgment of their behaviors for you, our readers. Our mission is to inform and inspire, not to degrade in any way. So please, even if you find what follows to be as repugnant as we do, remember that our efforts have been in the interest of science and the betterment of baseball and greater mankind.

While it would be futile to categorize each and every one of the millions of people who call themselves Yankee fans, we have outlined (at great personal effort and expense) some of the more typical Yankee fans that one is certain to encounter. After all, they are everywhere.

1. **The "Center of the Universe" Yankee Fan**—This group consists of aggressive, arrogant, and usually male Yankee fans who are unable to see signs of life beyond the Hudson River. Hailing from any of the five boroughs, but somehow most often from the Bronx, Queens, and Staten Island, these yahoos now live in exile from their beloved homeland and are found throughout the country, annoying the locals wherever they journey with endless babble about Yankee dominance, empirical superiority, and the belief that their Yankees have been somehow ordained by God to win all their championships, regardless of logical argument to the contrary.

   Although blameless for their place of birth, these fans are to be held completely responsible for their choice of teams (after all, they could become Mets fans). The "Center of the Universe" Yankee fans can be heard incessantly repeating condescending phrases like, "You got a nice little team down there in Florida, but remember the game of baseball belongs to the Yankees," or "Nearly triple the number of World Series Championships of the next closest ball club—and counting! End of argument!"

> I imagine rooting for the Yankees is like owning a yacht. —Jimmy Cannon

Yankee apologists will say that it's the New York way to be passionate about a sports team and that any other way of showing support would be half-hearted. If so, reason would suggest that the fans of other New York teams would be just as obnoxious. And they aren't. Nobody—not even other New Yorkers—beats the "Center of the Universe" Yankee fans in the obnoxious department.

KEVIN: Which fans would you rather hang out with and watch a game: Mets, Jets, Nets, Nicks, Islanders, Giants, Rangers, or Yankee fans?
JOSH: I think you know the answer to that.

2. **The New Yorker Wannabe**—These fans are, in fact, a subsection of the "Center of the Universe" fans, but they hail from New Jersey, Long Island, and southern Connecticut—though they are equally as obnoxious as their New York City brethren. The sole desire in life of Wannabes is to live in "The City" and own full-season boxes at Yankee Stadium. They

Wall Street bankers supposedly back the Yankees; Smith College girls approve of them. God, Brooks Brothers, and United States Steel are believed to be solidly in the Yankees' corner . . . The efficiently triumphant Yankee machine is a great institution—but, as they say, who can fall in love with U.S. Steel?
—Gary Talese in *There Are Fans—And Yankee Fans*

want so badly to be mistaken for New Yorkers that they are rarely found without the obligatory Yankee caps on over shaved heads or donning the pinstriped (home) jersey, ironically even in New Jersey.

Wannabes can be seen vomiting their way across River Avenue, after having consumed their weight in suds at one of the fine drinking establishments, on the way to the bleachers, where they can spend the entire game sneaking more booze, screaming obscenities at opposing players, and chastising Yankee players when they are less than perfect.

When confronted with arguments that question Yankee dominance, pride, or class, Wannabes respond with something like, "You are so freakin' jealous of all the Yankees' many championships and World Series rings that you can't even stand it. Deep down yous all wanna be Yankee fans."

As odd as it may seem, NY-Wannabes are far too afraid to actually use the public transportation of the city they so worship to get to the game and thus spend hours in their "totally bitchin'" IROC Camaros, blaring Springsteen on the ride home, after the three-hour Yankee post-game show has ended, of course.

KEVIN: Hey, I love Springsteen.
JOSH: And your family is teeming with Yankee fans. I'm beginning to wonder about you.

Police have arrested the man who was pictured throwing snowballs at Giants Stadium. If convicted, he may face six months in jail and a $1,000 fine. If it turns out he was under the influence of alcohol or drugs, he'll be signed by the Yankees.

—David Letterman

3. **The Yankee Jock Sniffer**—This particular variety of Yankee fan consists of males who were big fish in high school but have since fallen on harder times, athletically and socially. To reassert their prior dominance over others, Sniffers use the terms dweebs, dorks, and wusses to describe any non-Yankee fans. Sniffers rabidly support the teams in all sports that are most dominant and most likely to stay on top, thereby assuaging their failing egos. Perhaps the most unoriginal of thinkers among the Yankee fans, the Yankee Jock Sniffers thrive on being associated with the most winning team in sports history.

Sniffers' primary aspiration in life is to become the "Yankee Jock Sniffer Hanger-On," which is a typical Yankee Jock Sniffer who was fortunate enough to have gone to the same high school with a current Yankee player and is "in wit" the Yankee athlete tightly enough that he is allowed to "come over, hang out, and play X-Box" with his idol. Although many Yankee Jock Sniffers claim "Hanger-On" status, they are rare. Those who are truly Hangers-On often end up working security for their Yankee idol while he attends public functions. Most often, Sniffers can be seen herded up at the bar of some vacuous yuppie sports establishment pumping their fists in the air after watching another HGH-fueled Yankee home run on the YES network.

JOSH: A Sniffer I know got married wearing a pin-striped suit.
KEVIN: That doesn't sound that bad.
JOSH: The pinstripes were blue; the suit was white.
KEVIN: Ouch.

4. **Cutest-Yankee Female Fan**—"Oh my Gawd, Jeeta is so freakin' gorgeous!" and similar phrases will instantly identify this type of fan, and it is because Jeter is a Yankee that she dons the "NY" cap. As one caller to New York sports radio station WFAN observed, if you see a girl at a bar wearing a Mets cap, she can probably name most, if not all, of the players in the Mets' starting lineup. If you see a girl at a bar wearing a Yankees cap, she likely can name Jeter and A-Rod, and that's it. This type of fan believes that aesthetics is more important than athletics and that it is better not to slide so that her favorite player keeps his uniform looking good. Typically, the

"Cutest Yankee" fan ends up mated for life with a Yankee Jock Sniffer.

5. **Cutest-Yankee Male Fan**—For all intents and purposes, this category is completely interchangeable with the Cutest-Yankee Female Fan. The primary obsession of the Cutest-Yankee Male Fan is not with the ability or strategy of the sport and its players (like any real baseball fan), but rather with an individual player who looks best in his uniform or who hits the same New York clubs that Cutest-Yankee Male Fan does. Cutest-Yankee Male Fans have steadily increased within the broader ranks of Yankee fans—to epic proportions—with the arrival and success of Derek Jeter. (One can only suppose that a hairy, shabbily dressed, and beer-swilling Thurman Munson wasn't doing it for them.) With the acquisition of Alex Rodriguez, Cutest-Yankee Male Fans seem unconcerned with the quandary that having too many metrosexuals on the Yankee roster might negatively affect team chemistry.

You can take my cars or my house, just don't mess with my clothes.

—Alex Rodriguez

JOSH: Now, that's a ballplayer. He's a gamer, that one.
KEVIN: Best that money can buy.

6. **Po-Dunk America Yankee Fan**—These Yankee fans grow up in remote areas of the country that are not even

close to big league baseball—places like South Dakota, Arkansas, or Tampa. Living two days' drive from any MLB ballpark, these folks have the privilege of selecting any team in baseball to throw their support behind. And since the Yankees have the furthest reaching media, the dimmer and less original of the Po Dunks choose the Yankees and, for some reason that is as unknowable as how Paris Hilton became famous, seem to stick with their choice. Perhaps when they went to buy their first baseball cap, the Yankee cap was the only one available.

When the Yankee Stadium P.A. system plays Sinatra's "New York, New York" at the end of the game, Po Dunks can be seen tearing up when Old Blue Eyes croons the line, "These little town blues, are melting away."

As much as we disliked the Yankees, fans and players alike, they were good for baseball. The consistently unsuccessful teams, like the Browns, Senators, and A's, paid a lot of their bills with those big crowds that poured through the gates when the Yankees came to town.

—Bob Feller

7. **The Bandwagon Jumper**—The Bandwagon Jumper clings to whatever team happens to be on top at any particular point in time. "I've been a New York Yankees fan since I was six years old," Jumper is proud to proclaim as the Yankees approach the playoffs. Strangely, Jumper was eerily silent around New York during the Yankee drought of the '80s and early '90s.

However, a true Jumper will change colors faster than the Amazon Rainforest chameleon when another team starts to win. "I've been a Red Sox fan since I was five," Jumpers could be heard shouting in October 2004.

Caution: Do not confront Bandwagon Jumpers when their colors are changing. Although of low intelligence, they are vicious and will often attack when cornered out of self-defense, however logical or sound the reasoning of the opposing argument.

Jumpers are also easily identified by their attire: the blue and white Tar Heels or Blue Devils shorts that are so baggy that they resemble a long skirt dragging on the ground above $250 white basketball shoes that have never seen any court action, the oversized Yankee shirt with "Costanza" or, even more pathetic, their own name across the back, and the ubiquitous Yankee cap. It's not a pretty picture. This style of dress is usually reserved for thirteen-year-olds, but Jumper wears this uniform with pride.

JOSH: Perhaps this is what is meant by Yankee "Pride?"
KEVIN: Perhaps we're cornering the market on Yankee "snide."

Always root for the winner. That way you won't be disappointed.

—Tug McGraw

8. **The Baseball Neophyte**—These Yankee fans are frankly too green to realize that other baseball teams might

have storied traditions and histories, fully buying the media diet that they are force-fed (that the Yankees have had the only players in baseball worth mentioning). "Honus Wagner? He's no Babe Ruth," and "Stan Musial was a bum who couldn't have cut it in New York," are the types of things Neophyte might actually say.

The Baseball Neophyte can easily be confused with Bandwagon Jumper, as they appear very similar at first glance. However, just as the pupa transforms into the light-seeking moth, Neophytes who are indoctrinated at a young age with enough Yankee propaganda (one playoff game often contains sufficient Yankee bootlicking) can change into Wannabes or Po Dunks, whichever the case may be.

9. **The Euro-Trash Yankee Fan**—The Euro-Trash Yankee fan is the casual baseball fan on the continent of Europe who wears the Yankee cap (it might be the only ball team they know that exists) but who paradoxically disparages the evils of American culture, expansion, and excess at the same time. The Japanese variety of this fan is on the rise with Steinbrenner's marketing efforts having reached Asia as well. Euro-Trash Yankee fans are most often fans of Manchester United in soccer, unaware that the two enormously successful franchises have also formed a marketing partnership. This breed of fan seems unable to process the concept of irony.

10. **The "Plugging-My-Movie" Yankee Fan**—Perhaps the most vile and distasteful of all Yankee fans is the "Plugging-

My-Movie-or-TV-Show" variety. They are not fans of the game of baseball in the slightest or even fans of the Yankees in particular. One could assume that otherwise they might show up to a regular season game once in a while. But come playoff time, Pluggers score playoff tickets from their agents and don gratis Yankee garb in search of cheap camera photo-ops to promote their celebrity—especially the "Plugging-My-Reality-TV Show" variety. They are enabled tenfold by the FOX network in the promotion of their pathetic lineup of shows. We are led to believe by all-knowing FOX sportscasters that these celebrities can only break from the rigors of their schedule during the playoffs and that the sacrifice of their attendance proves them to be die-hard fans of the Bronx Bombers. Egregious examples have been the cast of *That 70s Show* and, of course, Donald Trump.

JOSH: But not Billy Crystal. He's obviously a fan, even if he supports an evil team.
KEVIN: At least he wore a Mets cap in *City Slickers*.

11. **The "Duped By Dad" Yankee Fan**—These sorry cases could have easily grown up to live their lives as fans of respectable teams, and developed baseball identities of their own. But tragically, early in life they were fed nonstop diets of Yankee propaganda by their fathers, mothers, uncles, or older cousins. Some scientists believe Dupers to be genetically predisposed to worshipping the Yankee cult, much the same way certain addictions can be chemically passed on from parent to child. And just as with

members of any other cult, intervention is often necessary, as these *true believers* have been brainwashed (sometimes by several generations) by the people they love and trust the most. The debriefing of a Duper can take years, and, sadly, some never fully recover.

After reading about the lowest and most depraved examples of Yankee fandom, some readers might be tempted to pity these poor Yankee saps. After all, we have compiled a rather unflattering, if painfully truthful, list. And we too might be inclined to feel some pity for these poor sods, if they weren't so infuriatingly vocal about how their Yankees are the only team in baseball to exhibit class, good sportsmanship, and pride. Remember the proverb, Yankee fans, "Pride goeth before the fall." In the minds of these misguided fans, there is room for only the Yankees and their heroics. How else can we explain the YES network? Don't attempt to confuse these fans with the idea that every story of Yankee greatness is not the absolute truth or that other teams have stories of greatness as well. These Yankee-lovers cannot decipher Yankee myth from Yankee reality. And their behavior follows in line, step by step, with members of other cults.

All we must do to determine how to treat these Yankee fans is to watch them in action. Trying to find bad fan behavior in the stands at Yankee Stadium is a bit like trying to find people wearing red bandannas at the annual running of the bulls in Pamplona. The sad part is that the actions of the bleacher creatures—and let's be honest, rabid and drunken Yankee fans in any other part of Yankee Stadium on any given night—are enough to make the argument rock solid. These fans call themselves the most loyal in all of sports. In actuality, the worst examples of Yankee fan behavior represent the lowest of the low, the bottom of the behavioral barrel: the constant booing (even of their own players), the inning-by-inning fights (and subsequent arrests) that folks stand and watch like cattle, the name-calling that extends beyond the clever and sarcastic and enters into the realm of psychopathic (and that's just the children), the pouring of beer, ketchup, and anything else handy onto the heads of opposing outfielders—all this we have come to expect as part of the Yankee Stadium experience.

To make matters worse, Yankee fans get drunk and disorderly, talk trash, and even threaten violence in every road stadium the Yankees visit (and sometimes when they're not even playing). Well, what can we expect from a team with players like Reggie Jackson and Graig Nettles, who got into a fight the night New York clinched the ALCS in 1981? While they talk of Yankee "pride" and "class," it is the disgraceful behavior of Yankee fans that most closely mirrors the actual state of the organization.

When events like these happen at other ballparks (and they certainly do), it makes the news. But the nightly shenanigans performed by Yankee fans on behalf of their beloved "greatest team in

> You see, the Mets are losers, just like nearly everybody else in life. This is the team for the cab driver who gets held up and the guy who loses out on a promotion because he didn't maneuver himself to lunch with the boss enough. It is the team for every guy who has to get out of bed in the morning and go to work for short money on a job he does not like. The Yankees? Who does well enough to root for them, Laurence Rockefeller?
> —Jimmy Breslin, in
> *Can't Anybody Here Play This Game?*

sports" is downright shameful. The sheer volume compelled us to leave off the below list such daily showing of affection by Yankee fans where they toss out onto the field golf balls, batteries, beer, shot glasses, walkmans, coins, and other debris. That is why we have compiled the Bottom Five Moments in Yankee Fandom History, for your enjoyment.

1. **September 10, 1961:** Two Yankee fans come out of the right field stands at Yankee Stadium to attack Cleveland centerfielder Jimmy Piersall during the seventh inning of the second game of a doubleheader. Piersall punches and kicks the two knuckleheads before teammates and police come to pull the men off. Note: This event occurred more than forty years before the attacks on Tom Gamboa in U.S. Cellular Field in Chicago.

2. **October 14, 1976:** In Game 5 of the ALCS against Kansas City, Chris Chambliss hits a home run that hands Yankee fans their first pennant in twelve years. What should have been a moment of Yankee glory turns into an ugly riot as hordes of Yankee fans storm the field, crowd the base paths, all to get a piece of Chambliss, in a scene straight out of the novel *Day of the Locust*. Chambliss later admits that he feared for his life as he attempted to circle the base paths among the mob of fans.

3. **August 27, 1986:** Wally Joyner, the first baseman of the California Angels is struck in the arm by a buck knife tossed down from the upper deck of Yankee Stadium. Although Joyner was not seriously injured, come on—it was a knife attack.

4. **October 4, 1995:** *After hitting two home runs in Game One of the ALDS in New York*, Yankee fans chant "Fuck you, Junior," to Seattle's Ken Griffey, Jr. during Game Two. Junior responds in the 12th inning with a towering home run that silences the crowd and puts the M's up 5–4. New York wins the game in the 15th inning, but the Mariners win three straight at home to take the series.

5. **October 20, 2004:** Game 6 of the ALCS against the Red Sox is delayed after A-Rod is ruled out for slapping the ball out of Bronson Arroyo's glove. Police in riot gear line the baselines at Yankee Stadium to dissuade fans from bringing the violence in the stands down onto the field.

Once again, what can you expect from the fans of a team whose idea of sportsmanship was displayed in all its finery when its leader, George Steinbrenner, punched the wall of an elevator (or something equally as hard) in 1981? The Yanks were losing to the Dodgers in the World Series, and Georgie apparently lost his cool. Of course, his version of the story is that he broke his hand punching the teeth out of two Dodger fans who had shown a lack of class and respect by calling the Yankees "chokers." So King George taught the two LA hooligans a lesson in class by "beating them up." If only that were the case. The Bad News Bears showed more class when they went to Japan. No lawsuits were ever filed against Steinbrenner, the Yankees, or anyone else, because the incident likely never happened as George reported it. But we suppose it's better for George to tell a little white lie about an event like this (which somehow doesn't boost his image, even if we believed it) than it is to just come clean and admit that he's a hothead who punched a wall out of frustration because he can't stand to lose. This is your leader, Yankee fans . . . this is the greatest owner in sports, as your legions have dubbed him.

And sadly, Yankee fans follow their "heroes" who are worthy of the "pride" and "honor" of wearing the Yankee uniform. They are quite simply as misguided and screwed up as their owner. Only they still haven't learned that about themselves. Well Yankee fans, the rest of America has. Forgive us if we're not impressed.

One night I was watching a quiz show on TV and the question was, "Name a baseball team synonymous with winning." One girl said, "Dodgers." The other girl said, "Giants." That made me madder than hell. I kept saying, "Yankees, you dummies." And of course the answer was the Yankees.
—Billy Martin

Chapter Eight

The Sad Case of Mr. Salvo

Josh here again, flashing back to my high school days, long before the Red Sox broke the "Curse of the Bambino" with their reverse sweep of the Yankees in the 2004 ALCS.

As I mentioned earlier, I'm a Yankee-hater just like my father was before me. I discovered in my youth, however, that my father dealt with his anti–New York emotions better than many fathers living in New England.

Growing up in rural Central Massachusetts, I attended a local grammar school, then headed off to a regional high school in a neighboring town. As such, I met a whole new cast of classmates in the ninth grade, and among them was a young man named Joe Salvo. Joe was almost as big a Red Sox fan as I was. The Red Sox were in the pennant race as our freshman year began, and Joe and I would "talk baseball" during algebra class by passing notes filled with statistics and theoretical batting orders back and forth across the rows of desks. We may have gotten C's in algebra, but we sure knew how to compute slugging percentages and earned run averages. Too bad it wasn't a statistics class.

Eventually Joe invited me to his house for a game of Wiffle ball, and I was happy to accept.

"There's only one thing," Joe told me as we got off the school bus at his house. "When my father gets home from work, whatever you do, make sure you don't mention the Yankees."

"What do you mean?" I asked.

"Please," Joe said, "Just don't mention the Yankees," and I could tell that whatever it was embarrassed him, so I didn't press him on the matter.

An hour later Mr. Salvo got home, parked his car in the garage, and walked across the lawn to say hello to Joe and to meet his new friend. Naturally, the conversation quickly came around to the fact that I was one of the biggest Red Sox fans at Shepherd Hill Regional High School, and naturally I couldn't resist mentioning that the Sox were in first place, and better yet, New York was in fourth.

I hadn't forgotten Joe's warning, but my curiosity got the better of me. I wanted to see what the big deal was about saying the word "Yankees" in front of Mr. Salvo, so I said, "The stupid Yankees."

No sooner than I had said the word, Mr. Salvo turned beet red. He glared at his son. Then, he looked at me and shook his head with a look of pure hatred on his face. He raised a quivering hand and pointed at me. "Maybe you use words like that at your house," he said, "but not here. *We* don't use that kind of language."

Then, Mr. Salvo turned and stomped across the lawn, got into his car and drove off, but not before nearly dropping his Aerostar's transmission in the driveway.

Joe, for his part, was already crying. When his mother got home from work half an hour later and heard about what had happened, her eyes too welled with tears. "We can only hope and pray he'll come through all right," she told her son. "Papa's in God's hands now."

At that point, I decided the prospect of finishing our Wiffle ball game was grim at best, so I telephoned my mother for a ride home. "I'll wait outside," I said.

In the days that followed I heard through the school grapevine that Mr. Salvo was missing, off on another one of his mysterious benders. For my role in this, I felt immensely guilty. I was therefore much relieved when Joe's father eventually returned, but it was a long time before Joe Salvo would pass Red Sox notes to me in class again. For several weeks whenever I sent him a new batting order, he would just crumple the piece of paper up and drop it on the floor without even looking at it.

After a while though, Joe forgave me and we became friends again. It was then that I learned that his father had been unable to hear the word "Yankees" without losing his wits ever since Bucky Dent's home run in the one-game playoff between the Yanks and Sox at Fenway Park in 1978. For this reason, Mr. Salvo's TV viewing of Red Sox games was limited to games against opponents other than the Yankees, and even then, he watched the games with the volume muted in case Sean McDonough or Bob Montgomery, the announcers, should happen to mention the scores from around the league and utter the unmentionable name. Whenever Mr. Salvo did hear the word, or even inadvertently thought about the Yankees, he suffered something akin to a nervous breakdown and disappeared for a few days, or sometimes even weeks. Joe and his mother didn't know where he went or what he did during his time away. They only knew that when he eventually came home, he was "okay" again, at least until his next episode.

For the remainder of my high school years, whenever I needed to reference the Yankees while visiting the House of Salvo, I referred to the team as the "American League New York franchise," just as Joe did. But it didn't matter. My acquiescence, I would later find out, only delayed the inevitable.

After graduation, Joe and I drifted apart. But I ran into my old friend one night at an arena football game in Worcester, Massachusetts. We exchanged the usual array of long-time-no-see pleasantries and lamented the latest Red Sox foibles. Joe's mood became somber though when the topic turned to how our respective families were doing. Sensing that something was wrong, I asked Joe if his father was still struggling with his American League New York franchise-related episodes, and he said, "No."

"So he's finally gotten over the Dent homer?" I asked.

"Not exactly," Joe said, then he burst into tears, just as he had so many times during our high school days, and ran off to the nearest men's room to compose himself.

Later that night we sat side by side at a downtown bar, both doing our part to drown poor Joe Salvo's sorrows. He told me everything. Unbeknownst to him and his mother, his father had lived a double life for years. In addition to the family home in Dudley, Massachusetts, Mr. Salvo had also maintained a studio apartment in the South Bronx. When his father disappeared, Joe told me, he would go to the apartment.

"Bizarre," I said. "He would go right into the heart of Yankee Country." I thought about this for a moment then suggested, "Perhaps it was a way of confronting his demons?"

"Wait," Joe told me. "There's more."

And there was more, much more.

Shortly after Mr. Salvo was committed to the mental institution, Joe explained, he and his mother had learned of his getaway lair and traveled to New York City to clean out the apartment and retrieve his belongings. "It was unbelievable," Joe said. "The walls were covered with Yankee pennants, posters, and autographed pictures. There were eight-by-ten photos of Reggie Jackson, Billy Martin, George Steinbrenner, Thurman Munson—the whole crew. There was even a picture of Bucky Dent celebrating at home plate after his homer in the playoff game. The dresser drawers were stuffed with Yankee T-shirts, jerseys, and pinstriped boxer shorts, and there was a hat rack in the closet full of fitted Yankees caps in all styles matching my father's hat size. We found old ticket stubs and game programs in another drawer—hundreds of them. My father, it seemed, preferred to sit in the right field bleachers with the most ardent Yankee fans of all. We found many of their names in an address book on his nightstand."

"Wow," I said. "That's some alter ego. I've heard about men who keep extra wives and families on the side, but never baseball teams."

"My father was a very sick man," Joe said. "Do you know what the strangest thing was, though?"

"No," I said. "What?"

"Well," Joe said. "As I stood in that apartment surrounded by Yankee memorabilia, I couldn't help but feel a little bit tingly."

I asked Joe what he meant by "tingly."

"You know," he said, smiling nervously, "I couldn't help but feel a little bit awed by the Yankees' great history and mystique. I mean, all of those famous Yankees in the pictures were staring at me, and there were pinstriped pajamas spilling out of the drawers. I could feel the tradition and the pride, and it made me feel, you know, like a winner must feel."

As I sat at the bar listening to my old friend babble about Yankee tradition and pride, the moment was quickly becoming one of those surreal snapshots in time that I would never forget—kind of like being in a car crash or being dumped by a girlfriend. I could see what was coming, but I had no way of stopping it. So I just sat there listening.

"I couldn't help myself," Joe said, flashing another timid smile. "I just had to do it."

"Do what?" I asked, cringing.

"I tried on one of the hats," Joe said. "And one of the T-shirts . . . and a pair of boxers. You know, just to see how they would feel."

My old friend sat beside me at the bar smiling with these crazy eyes. Then as soon as it had come over him, the spell seemed to pass, and he was himself again.

"I guess it was just a crazy phase I went through," Joe said.

It was one of the saddest moments of my life. I stood up, pushed in my stool, told the barkeep that "the Yankee fan" would be picking up the tab, and walked away. As much as I hated to abandon a friend in need, I knew that there was no twelve-step plan to cure what ailed him. His soul had already been lost.

They got our parents, and now the sons of bitches are coming to get us.
—Anonymous Red Sox fan before the 1978 one-game playoff between Boston and New York

Chapter Nine

Yankee Pride, Yankee Arrogance

The term "Yankee Pride" is thrown around in the media and among Yankee fans more frequently than the rumors of which "lucky" gal is dating Derek Jeter. We are told that Yankee Pride is a special brand of pride that encompasses being a class act both on and off the field and always giving your best effort. All teams wish to mimic it, all players desire to have it, but they cannot. Only by playing for the Yankees can a player be considered worthy. Even Cal Ripken, Jr., as hard as he played throughout his career, only did so in imitation of Yankee greats, the class of the sporting world.

Or so we are told.

We don't buy this load of malarkey for a minute, so we decided to investigate the history and tradition of so-called Yankee Pride, all through the eras from its inception, in the attempt to find the most valiant and pride-hearted Yankee of them all. We thought that if pride is indeed a real and tangible commodity unique to the Yankees to such a degree that they can rightfully base a franchise mythology on it, then certainly we should be able to find the stuff in abundance when looking at the Yankees' star players.

So, we wondered if it was Babe Ruth who embodied Yankee Pride best, with his ability to transform both the game and nation. Or perhaps it was Lou Gehrig, for his sheer will and determination to keep on playing through pain, game after agonizing game. Certainly any discussion of pride must include Joe DiMaggio, who played his heart out every day. When asked why he always played so hard, the Yankee Clipper replied:

Because there might be somebody out there who's never seen me play.

—Joe DiMaggio

Now that's what we call pride. Never mind that Joltin' Joe has been accused in recent biographies of having lived his life very differently off the baseball diamond—abusive and neglectful toward his children, disdainful of the fans, and a cheapskate to boot. While we considered looking at actions on the field only, the Yankee spotlight shines so brightly on Yankee players both on and off the field that we decided we simply must include all we know about a Yankee when determining the winner of our coveted prize of YEMP (Yankee Embodying the Most Pride).

JOSH: Sounds a little like Shemp, the fourth of the Three Stooges.
KEVIN: Mo, Curly, and Larry . . . and YEMP; that's some Murderers' Row.

And that being the case, we decided to toss out the great Joltin' Joe DiMaggio. He was a great player no doubt, but he has more unauthorized biographies doing him harm than Michael Jackson.

Next, we considered Yogi Berra. Everyone likes Yogi, right? And though Yogi has won more World Series rings than any other player in history, his main contribution to baseball has been his colorful use of . . . whatever language it is that Yogi speaks. Actually, we love Yogi's colorful (mis)use of the language and agree with Yankees fans that Berra is quite a character. When he was honored at "Yogi Berra Night" at Sportsman Park in St. Louis, Yogi spouted this gem:

I'm a lucky guy and I'm happy to be with the Yankees. And I want to thank everyone for making this night necessary.

—Yogi Berra

He's kind of like that crazy uncle that makes you laugh at holiday dinners but who you duck when you spot him in the supermarket because you just know he's going to embarrass you. And once the kind and venerable Yogi got so angry at his beloved Yankee organization that he vowed never to return to Yankee Stadium as long as Steinbrenner was at the helm. While we give kudos to Yogi for the courage of his convictions (even though he has since returned with Steinbrenner still fully in charge), he spent many years flirting with the kind of hatred that we share for the chief Yankee of them all. Can't say that we blame him for not feeling the "Pride of the Yankees" while Stein is in charge. But you don't quit midseason, then come back looking to win the MVP (or YEMP) award.

Of course, Mickey Mantle must also enter into any discussion concerning Yankee greats exemplifying pride. Many of those who saw him play said Mantle's raw talent far exceeded that of any other player they had seen previously or have seen since. Great credentials. However, the same folks often accuse "The Mick" of applying his talent in a rather casual manner. Teammate Gene Woodling had this to say:

> You know, Mantle had the greatest ability of any guy who ever came to the big leagues in my time. He didn't have to apply himself. He didn't realize how good he was . . . If he'd have been a little more on determination, like DiMaggio. DiMaggio was a very determined guy, you know. Mantle could have set unbelievable records. He only used about three-quarters of his talent.
>
> —Eugene Richard Woodling

Undoubtedly, Mantle is one of the greatest players to ever step foot in Yankee Stadium. But if criticisms are true that he only gave 75 percent (and there are many who say this), he can hardly be considered the player who epitomized the pride of an entire franchise. Giving 100 percent is bare minimum, as Yankee fans have told us.

It was immediately after Mantle's era that we noticed a severe decline in this supposed Yankee Pride, as we evaluated the Yankees generation by generation. Truly, how can one put Reggie Jackson on the same list as these other men? Despite his October pedigree, the man's own words speak more about his character than we could.

> After Jackie Robinson the most important black in baseball history is Reggie Jackson, I really mean that.
>
> —Reggie Jackson

Don't suppose the names Mays or Aaron mean anything to you, do they Reggie? How about Willie McCovey or Bob Gibson? Ringing any bells? Not to mention the enormous insult a comment like Jackson's tosses toward Satchel Page, Josh Gibson, and the scores of other players who excelled in the Negro Leagues. Let's face facts: Mr. October is little more than a conceited jackass who struck out more than any other player in history.

JOSH: He's no YEMP, not in my book.
KEVIN: Maybe *he's* Shemp?

Yankee manager Billy Martin was no friend to Reggie, even if Jackson did have a candy bar named after him. This fact alone is an enormous plus in our book. Martin never got on too well with Jackson, and that created some very interesting years in the Bronx, as chronicled in Sparky Lyle's *The Bronx Zoo*. But Billy's resolve that he himself represented Yankee Pride seems just as ludicrous as the notion that Jackson could. On Martin's tombstone, it is written:

> I may not have been the greatest Yankee to put on the uniform, but I was the proudest.
>
> —Billy Martin

The thing is, Martin just wasn't that good of a Yankee player. And he was traded away from the Yankees after embarrassing the team by getting in a bar fight on his birthday at the Copacabana nightclub in 1957. In fact, Martin drank and fought his way through both his careers as a player and manager. Nothing to be proud of there. And as Yankee manager, Billy was fired or forced to resign five times. Perhaps these are not the best credentials for the pinnacle of Yankee pride.

> All I know is, I pass people on the street these days, and they don't know whether to say hello or to say good-bye.
>
> —Billy Martin

But in Billy's defense, he did have to work under the megalomaniacal George Steinbrenner. Since we've taken enough pot shots at George already, we'll let his favorite ex-employee do the talking for us.

> What does George [Steinbrenner] know about Yankee pride? When did he ever play for the Yankees?
>
> —Billy Martin

Good point, Billy. Yankee fans agree that if Steinbrenner's behavior is something to be proud of, then the Back Street Boys were misunderstood musical geniuses. And since Ruth spent most of his time off the field either drunk or carousing (and some of his time on the field doing the same), we'll pass on him for the YEMP as well. Plus, he was a great Red Sox player first, and no former Red Sox player can truly embody Yankee pride. Guess that argument leaves Roger Clemens, Wade Boggs, and a long list of other players out of the running as well.

Thurman Munson, God rest his soul, typifies more than any other Yankee of the era the combative Bronx Zoo mentality that Lyle chronicled. A notoriously tough competitor and prickly personality, Munson was known to spit tobacco juice at fans while signing autographs—at least the fans he suspected were selling the autographs for cash. Not the most glorious or proud chapter in Yankee history, to be sure.

How about the new guys? At first glance, Derek Jeter seems to be a better than average player and a fairly classy guy—if looks, brains, and talent don't count for anything. But just how much class is there in Jeter when he's not even the best shortstop (hitting or fielding) on his own team, much less in the American League? Yet Jeter insists on staying put at shortstop, when his team could certainly be improved with another player in that position. His actions can be classified as nothing less than detrimental to his team. Talk about arrogance. And even with the obvious Yankee counterargument that by staying at short and having A-Rod play third the team chemistry improves, on-field greatness is mandatory for the YEMP award. And A-Rod is still a better hitting and fielding shortstop than Jeter.

Another guy Yankee fans tried to will toward greatness was Don Mattingly, so much so that he was deified with the nickname "Donnie Baseball." But again, the fact is that no matter how you slice it, Mattingly was a solid first bagger, but doesn't have Hall of Fame numbers. How can we give the YEMP award to a guy who has thirty-nine guys from his own team ahead of him in the Hall of Fame? The Yankees never won a World Series in the Mattingly era either, and they suffered the worst offensive collapse in playoff history in Donnie Baseball's first year as batting coach, losing the American League Championship Series to the 2004 Red Sox in four straight games, after being up 3–0. His players' bats went colder than Steinbrenner's heart, and he could do nothing to revive them. Nope, Donnie Baseball is out.

So who does that leave in the running? Looks like a one-horse race, the Iron Horse, Lou Gehrig. Okay, Yanks fans, just to show we're charitable, we'll grant you this one player. Lou Gehrig has earned the moniker Pride of the Yankees. (Seems kind of obvious in retrospect, doesn't it?)

But you must admit, there's not a lot there, is there? Embarrassingly little considering how often we must endure the blathering on and on about it from Yankee fans and the press. Certainly there's not enough there to base an entire franchise mythology on. Bush had more to go on when he went looking for weapons of mass destruction. The rest is, as they say, creative story telling.

For your further entertainment, we have compiled a list of the most egregious examples of Yankee pride gone utterly sour. Drumroll, please:

THE TEN LOWEST MOMENTS IN YANKEE PRIDE HISTORY

10. George Steinbrenner is twice suspended from baseball—once for his illegal dealings in the Watergate scandal and once for his attempts to pin false allegations on his own right fielder, Dave Winfield. Winfield was Steinbrenner's own player, yet Stein had grown disenchanted with the star right fielder and was charged with hiring gambler Howie Spira to dig up dirt about Winfield's life off the field, in attempts to reneg on his contract. And why did Stein do all this? Because Winfield wasn't living up to King George's notion of Yankee Pride and a little miscalculation by George in the cost of living raise in Winfield's contract.

I won't be active in the day-to-day operations of the ball club at all.

—George Steinbrenner, 1973, after buying the Yankees

9. Graig Nettles corks his bat in a game against the White Sox, then comes up with a pathetic excuse to cover up what he did.

It was the first time I used that bat. A Yankee fan in Chicago gave it to me the last time we were there and said it would bring me luck. There's no brand name on it or anything. Maybe the guy made it himself. It had been in the bat rack, and I picked it up by mistake because it looked like the bat I had been using the last few days.

—Graig Nettles

This kind of behavior should have tipped off Yankee fans that there was something rotten at the center of their false myth of Yankee Pride. But it did not. Nettles is remembered as a Yankee great because he was on a championship team, not for cheating and then lying to cover it up.

8. David "Boomer" Wells after being invited into a sacred baseball shrine writes "Fenway Sucks" on the wall inside the scoreboard of the Green Monster in the moments before the 1999 All-Star Game.

JOSH: Classy move, Boomer. You show such reverence and respect for the game.
KEVIN: And then he became a Red Sox pitcher. Pitiful.

7. Alex Rodriguez sissy slaps Bronson Arroyo's glove during the sixth game of the 2004 ALCS, in a pathetic attempt to knock the ball loose when he was

out by ten feet. Then A-Rod whines to the umpire who called him out, saying that it was just the normal motion of his arm while running.

I want to step forward. I don't want to step on anyone's toes doing it. If I do, too bad.

—Alex Rodriguez

KEVIN: I've seen schoolgirls play the game with more class than this bozo.
JOSH: Saying that is an insult to schoolgirls . . . and clowns. And speaking of schoolgirls:

6. Luis "I thought she was seventeen" Polonia is convicted of statutory rape in 1989 for which he serves time. That doesn't prevent him for playing left field for the Yanks, though, after he gets out of the hoosegow.

JOSH: Yet another fine example of Yankee pride and class.
KEVIN: Double ouch.

5. Roger Clemens makes comments about Hank Aaron after the latter suggests that pitchers should not be eligible for the Most Valuable Player award.

I wish he were still playing. I'd probably crack his head open to show him how valuable I was.

—Roger Clemens

KEVIN: I guess for a true competitor like Roger, the Cy Young Award just isn't enough.

JOSH: Man, am I ever enjoying this list.

4. Steve Howe racks up seven lifetime suspensions for violation of baseball's drug policies.

This should have been the harbinger to us all of the league's failed drug policies to come. But instead, Howe is given a slap on the wrist, just like the "five strikes and you're still not quite out yet" steroid policy, which the league begrudgingly instituted in 2004. Delay in instituting a steroid policy that's weaker than circus lemonade could only result in:

3. Jason Giambi and Gary Sheffield—the heart of the Yankee hitting order at the time—admit to a Grand Jury that they used illegal steroids.

Although Sheffield's admission that he used illegal steroids "unknowingly" is laughable, we have to wonder why Yankee fans and their media stooges vilify Giambi but are giving Sheffield a free ride.

KEVIN: Could it be because Giambi told the truth (sort of—he apologized profusely for doing something wrong, but never actually mentioned the words "I used steroids," except to the Grand Jury) and Sheffield just flat out lied about it?

JOSH: More likely it's because Sheffield had a good year and Giambi stunk it up.

KEVIN: When wins become more important than character, on an all-new *Oprah*.

It's interesting how on Giambi's return to the game in 2005 after a miserable 2004 campaign, he received a standing ovation from the crowd, a better reception than players who've played hard and kept their noses clean all along, like Bernie Williams and Jorge Posada—even Jeter. Could it be that Yankee fans want Giambi to succeed so that Yankee critics will be silenced, rather than concerning themselves with whether Yankee players are obeying the rules in the first place?

2. Billy Martin and Reggie Jackson get in a fistfight in the visiting dugout at Fenway Park after Martin yanks Jackson from a game when he dogs a play in right field.

These two flunkees deserved the time they spent antagonizing each other. And we miss their on- (and off-) field antics and the sad state of the Yankee era it all represented. It may not have been pride-filled—even to the most die-hard Yankee apologists—but at least it was more entertaining than watching the Yankees coast to another AL East title.

And at the bottom, the absolute lowest moment in Yankee history is:

1. Roger Clemens throws a bat fragment at Mike Piazza during the 2000 World Series, then serves up this lame excuse:

I thought it was the ball.

Roger, Roger, Roger. Just admit what you did. Twenty million people watched you try to intimidate your way into history by throwing a splintered chunk of wood at a player who has owned you at the plate. Your behavior was tantamount to Mike Tyson's ear-biting incident. If you pulled a stunt like this on the street corner outside the ballpark, you would have been arrested. If it was anywhere else other than on TV (in the World Series, no less) Piazza might have been justified in kicking your bully butt. But no, the media covered you once again by saying things like, "See, Roger is an intense competitor who *must have lost track of what he was doing* because he'd gotten himself so far in the competitive zone."

Save it.

We're not saying that other power pitchers don't use intimidation as a tactic. Pitching with power means *owning* the strike zone, so a high-and-tight one once in a while is—without question—part of the game. Everyone above Little League knows this and makes adjustments for it.

But you crossed the line severely, Roger, and you should have been honest about it and admitted publicly that you behaved like a classless jackass. You may be among the top ten pitchers of all time, but antics like this will get you a reputation of being a Ty Cobb disciple. So admit you were a jerk, and we'll move you on our list of All Time Low Points in Yankee Pride, down to say No. 4 or No. 5. But don't insult our intelligence by claiming you thought a shard of broken bat was a baseball. Not being able to tell the difference just makes you look stupid. And even if it was the ball, why would you throw it at the base runner? This isn't kickball, genius; it's the big leagues. You throw to first base. But we suspect you already know that. And that's why you're at the bottom of our list. A very special "Bronx Cheer" goes out, from us, especially to you.

Rather than giving you a much deserved beating on national TV, it seems as though Piazza may have found a way to get back at you during the 2004 All-Star game, where, somehow, your dominance of the first half of the NL season evaporated in a matter of seconds. Opening the game—perhaps courtesy of Mr. Piazza starting as catcher—you got rocked. Could your catcher have been, say, tipping off the hitters as to what pitch was coming? We're not making any accusations. (Maybe we've seen *Bull Durham* one too many times.) We're merely speculating as to why you got pounded so hard. And we suspect that not even you could blame Piazza (if he indeed did this), because you knew you had it coming. Because you know in your heart of hearts just how wrong you on that fateful October day, when you threw the heavy end of a broken bat at another player. We're willing to call it even if you are, but never have we seen a more classless act on a baseball diamond, at any level.

There's something very, very wrong with these Yankees and with our society for focusing too much on a false notion of "Pride" and for too quickly forgetting incidents like these.

We're putting out a challenge to anyone to find a team that has more incidences of deplorable behavior than the Yankees of the last thirty years. (Oakland doesn't count.) In fact, we suspect that the Yankees can outdo all of baseball for deplorable examples of low-class behavior (and we don't even have to use the examples of poor fan behavior, which we've saved for another chapter), the same way that Ruth single-handedly hit more home runs in 1920 (fifty-four) than any other AL team totaled that year. Whatever remains of the Yankee pride that was typified by Gehrig has most certainly been shredded, burned, and buried under second base during the George Steinbrenner era.

And so, we give the YEMP award to Lou Gehrig who played the game in a simpler time, played every day, but is perhaps the only quality Yankee player who truly left a legacy that all baseball fans can respect. Truly, Gehrig should have considered himself the "luckiest man alive" to have played during a long ago era of Yankee history, and not with the parcel of jackasses that Steinbrenner has run out onto the field in recent years.

Chapter Ten

No Day at the Ballpark

Josh here again. Being a Red Sox fan, there have naturally been a slew of Yankee-related low points in my life. But one incident still leaves a particularly sour aftertaste in my mouth—much like the food at Yankee Stadium.

The date was June 19, 2000, and for the first and only time in my life I had a *miserable* time at the ballpark. To understand how profound an occurrence this was, you need to understand that my very existence as a fan is predicated on the belief that any day at the ballpark is special, and that goes doubly for any day spent at Fenway Park. Ordinarily, even when the Sox lose, I can appreciate the sights and sounds and smells of the old ball yard. But this day was different.

The Red Sox entered the series still vying for the AL East title. And I was sure my heroes were going to send the Yanks home with a string of losses.

As usual, I arrived at Fenway about four hours before the first pitch, which meant I had about two and a half hours to kill before the gates opened. I made the most of my spare time by milling around on Landsdowne Street, waiting for batting practice homers to fly over the Green Monster and by treating myself to one delicious grilled sausage after another.

When the ballpark finally opened, I hurried to my usual spot in the bleachers where I like to watch BP at field level in Fenway's center-field triangle. Okay, I'll be honest—more than just *watching* batting practice, I participate in it in my own way. I wait for long fly balls to land in Fenway's famous triangle, and when they bounce into the stands I scramble, competing with other slightly deranged fans, to collect them. The kid in me still loves to go home from the game with a ball. One of my regular ball hawking strategies is to brownnose the visiting team's pitchers as they shag balls during BP. When a player comes into the triangle in pursuit of a ball, I might casually say, "Nice day for a ball game, isn't it?" Then, very politely, I say, "How 'bout it? Can you spare a ball? Please." Sometimes this works, other times the player simply ignores me.

In any case, a certain Yankee relief ace was shagging flies in center field on this particular evening. Well, not exactly shagging them. He was mostly lollygagging after balls after they dropped rather than trying to catch them, and I remember thinking that the Big Stein would have surely disapproved of such half-hearted and unprofessional shagging. And besides, his hair was in need of a trim. But just the same, I was pleasant to the slender pinstriped pitcher when he eventually made his way into the triangle to retrieve a ball that had trickled past him.

"Hey, ——," I said, calling the reliever by his preferred Yankee nickname, but making no effort to disguise the fact that I was a Red Sox fan (Sox hat, "Reverse the Curse" T-shirt, my Boston accent).

"Nice day for a game," I said.

The Yankee looked at me for an instant but issued no reply.

"You sure are off to another great start," I said. "As a Red Sox fan, I hate to see it, but you're really mowing 'em down."

The pitcher squinted. Then he bent down to pick up the baseball.

"How 'bout it?" I said. "How 'bout a ball? It would make my day."

"A ball for you? Sure," the pinstriped Pinocchio said.

I held up my glove and he flipped the ball in my direction. But his throw came up short. It hit the top of the outfield fence and fell down to the warning track.

"Missed that one," I said sheepishly.

"No problem," he said. "Try again."

And sure enough, the pitcher retrieved the ball to give me another shot. He turned back toward the field and tossed the ball behind his back, again in my direction. But again the ball came within inches of my reach, hitting the top of the wall and then falling back to the field.

"You want to try again?" the Yankee called. By now, I could barely believe it, he was actually hustling to pick up the ball and give it another toss.

It took four failed attempts—probably a few more than it should have—for me to realize that the pride of the Yankees' bullpen was having a bit of fun at my expense. He was getting his sadistic jollies out of watching me—a grown man—lunge for a baseball that I had no chance of reaching. Eventually, when I figured out what was going on, he tossed the ball toward second base and ran back to his position in center field where he continued to languidly watch balls roll past him.

By the time my wife, Heather, got out of work and arrived at the park to meet me, I was shouting at my new enemy that his Yankees were going to lose big and that I'd be laughing all night long as the Red Sox put him and his obnoxious teammates in their place.

"What's gotten into you?" Heather asked. "You don't usually heckle players."

I told her how I'd been teased by the loafing Yankee.

"What a jerk," she said. "But don't let him ruin your day."

"Don't worry," I said. "He hasn't ruined anything. The sun is shining, I'm at Fenway Park, I've got a belly full of processed pork, and in one hour the Red Sox are going to show these louts from New York who's boss. Let's play ball."

The Red Sox played ball, all right . . . for three innings. After that, they looked as pathetic as I must have looked lunging for those pregame tosses. The game was scoreless until the top of the fourth inning when the Yankees scored three runs against Boston starter Brian Rose, including two on a Jorge Posada homer that flew right over my head. In the fifth the Yankees added two more on a Derek Jeter dinger, and in the sixth they added another. But I was still hopeful when the Sox scored a run in the seventh to make it 6–1.

"You see that, ———?" I yelled, though the reliever was 150 feet away in the Yankees' bullpen. "I smell a comeback!"

But there was to be no comeback. The Yankees scored nine runs against Rob Stanifer in the eighth and seven more against Tim Wakefield in the ninth. The final score was 22–1. It was the second-worst loss in Red Sox history, and the most runs scored by the Yankees since 1953.

While thousands of Red Sox fans headed home early, Heather and I stayed until the last out. My father hadn't raised me to leave games early. After the game mercifully ended, we stood staring at the scoreboard in disbelief as fans trickled toward the exits.

"The Red Sox could have hit five grand slams in the ninth," Heather said, "and they still would have lost."

"Pathetic," I agreed.

Just then, as the Yankee relievers filed out of the visiting bullpen, I saw a slender pinstriped figure running along the warning track toward center field. It happened so fast. First, I saw the ball in his hand. Next I saw it coming toward me. I fumbled with my glove. I reached out. And then, "Thud," the ball smacked against the top of the wall and fell humiliatingly to the warning track once again. My nemesis cackled heartily before jogging to catch up with the gaggle of relievers walking toward the Yankees' dugout.

"He fooled me again," I said, staring at the ball on the dirt track.

"Yes, fooled again," Heather said, still staring at the scoreboard.

It wasn't bad enough that the Yankees had beaten my team, but one of their players had also gone out of his way to make a schmuck out of me personally. My hatred for the Yankees doubled, or maybe even tripled, that day, and it has continued growing ever since.

The more self-centered and egotistical a guy is, the better ballplayer he's going to be. You take a team with twenty-five assholes and I'll show you a pennant. I'll show you the New York Yankees.
—Bill Lee

Chapter Eleven

The Axis of Baseball Evil— It Wasn't Always This Way

Writing a book about hating the Yankees is a dream come true for us. Not only do we get to rail on a team that is leading the charge toward the destruction of baseball as we know it (in the same way that *Queer Eye for the Straight Guy* has decimated the perfectly reasonable idea that being a regular slovenly guy is normal behavior), but we also get paid to spout off our opinions. We feel truly blessed. When we sat down to try to find ways to humiliate, disparage, point fingers at, and generally expose the ugly truth about the Yankees, we wanted to hit all eras of the game.

> **JOSH:** No Yankee is a good Yankee, I always say.
> **KEVIN:** Here, here.

Admittedly, our attitude toward the Bronx Bombers was rancorous and fueled by our own hatred—and not entirely by the facts. We wanted to smear Ruth and DiMaggio, Mantle and Gehrig alike, right alongside Jeter, Jackson, and Clemens. Trouble was, we couldn't do it. We were stunned to discover that we actually like the Yankees of old. Well, some of them.

> **KEVIN:** "Like" might be too strong a word.
> **JOSH:** How about "don't despise?"

To be fair, however, we must ask all of our Yankee-hating brethren to put themselves through the same rigorous gut-check that we've gone through, and to ask themselves this question: What in the world is there to hate about Lou Gehrig?

> **JOSH:** He wore pinstripes and played in New York?
> **KEVIN:** So does Mike Piazza.
> **JOSH:** Right. And he hates Clemens, so he's a friend of mine.

It's a tough question, isn't it? After all, Gehrig single-handedly set new standards for the qualities of commitment and team loyalty as he played through the excruciating pain of the disease that now bears his name. And then he got up in front of that microphone to announce his retirement, and damn it if he wasn't a hell of a nice guy on top of it all.

> **So I close in saying that I may have had a tough break, but I have an awful lot to live for. Thank you.**
>
> **—Lou Gehrig, at the end of his actual retirement speech**

> People all say that I've had a bad break, but today . . . today,
> I consider myself the luckiest man on the face of the earth.
>
> —Gary Cooper, as Lou Gehrig in *Pride of the Yankees*

Okay, so the Hollywood writers rearranged Gerhig's speech a bit so that Cooper could deliver the most powerful and dramatic part of his speech last. But should that matter? We can still hear the echoes bouncing off the façade of old Yankees Stadium, ringing in our ears. "LUCKIEST MAN . . . luckiest man . . . —iest man . . . ON THE FACE . . . on the face . . . the face . . . OF THE EARTH . . . of the earth . . . the earth." It's haunting. Anyone who doesn't respect Gehrig doesn't respect baseball.

And what about Babe Ruth? Sure the guy drank like Dean Martin and womanized like Wilt Chamberlain. Sure his appetites for food and life were huge. Sure he loved the spotlight and made a buffoon of himself in front of the camera to boost his growing image to the status of an American icon. But Ruth grew up in an orphanage and stayed late after games to sign autographs for kids. It wasn't a publicity stunt either; Ruth honestly cared about kids and never forgot the humble background from whence he came. Anyone who doesn't respect Ruth doesn't respect the American Dream.

> Best player ever? I'd have to go with the immoral Babe Ruth.
>
> —Johnny Logan

And while opinion seems split on Mickey Mantle and Joe DiMaggio, by most accounts "The Mick" and "Joltin' Joe" were well-liked by the fans, reporters, and their teammates, and even most opposing players had few negative words to say about them. And there's no denying that these men were among the very best to play the game during their eras.

> **What can you say about Mickey after you say he was one of the greatest? He had talent he didn't realize he had. If he had DiMaggio's serious bear-down attitude, there's no telling how great he could have been. With his one good leg, he could outrun everyone.**
>
> **—Gene Woodling**

So it seems that these Yankee greats were decent enough human beings, if slightly rough around the edges. The point is that they were easy for most Americans to relate to. DiMaggio was the son of an immigrant Italian fisherman. Ruth was an orphan who never lost his love of life and kids, and Mick was the type of fun-loving country boy you might have a beer with at a corner bar in smalltown Oklahoma. In their own ways, they were all underdogs in society originally—like a lot of ballplayers and Americans at the time.

So just when precisely (you must certainly be asking yourself) did the Yankee organization morph into the abomination that it is today? How could these great Yankees of old—the great Murderers' Row, with Yanks like Gehrig, Ruth, Bob Meusel, and Tony Lazzeri, and pitchers like Waite Hoyt and Urban Shocker, along with those of the era of the 1950s where New York City dominated the baseball landscape—turn bad? When did Yankees players devolve into the mercenary, money grubbing, entitled prima donnas that we see donning Yankee uniforms today?

> **It's great to be young and a Yankee.**
>
> **—Waite Hoyt**

The will to win is worthless if you don't get paid for it.

—Reggie Jackson

At nighttime, you just try to keep him [David Wells] out of jail.

—David Cone

Looks aren't the number one thing. They [players] have to have class, intelligence, then looks. If I was the ugliest SOB in the world it would be a lot easier.

—Alex Rodriguez

Well, we're pleased that you asked.

It comes down to a phrase: the Axis of Baseball Evil, which we have liberally borrowed and modified slightly from President G.W. Bush, who himself borrowed it (perhaps unknowingly) from the evil Axis Powers of Germany, Italy, and Japan during WWII. Dubya's Axis consisted of Iraq, Iran, and North Korea. Perhaps not so coincidentally, the Axis of Baseball Evil also has three supportive stakes, much like a teepee. Pull one of these three axes out and the whole teepee falls down. This obviously isn't so with Dubya's Axis, but we'll leave politics out of our discussion for now.

The first axis in the Axis of Baseball Evil is the seemingly un-limited resources that the New York media market has always pro-vided. The Yankees enjoyed the biggest revenues from attendance in the days before television. More than six major New York and sur-rounding area newspapers regaled the deeds of Ruth to the world. When the farm systems existed to develop talent for use within the organization, rather than merely to produce trade bait, the Yankees used their cash advantage to build an unparalleled scouting and player development empire. When not even that farm system proved to be enough of an advantage, the Yankees bought players from the Kansas City A's in an unholy and underhanded silent agreement that smacks so egregiously of collusion that when it is viewed in hindsight it makes the Iran-Contra Affair pale by comparison.

Then in 1958, after the two other teams that called New York home pulled up stakes and headed for the West Coast, the Yankees, for the first time in baseball's history, stood alone atop the mountain of media and merchandise money that was the biggest market the continent had to offer. The Giants and Dodgers had forsaken the city forever, and the Yankees were there to pick up the pieces. And even if the Mets were brought in a few years later to appease Senior Circuit fans, the Mets have never enjoyed income streams comparable to the Yankees. Comparing the Yankees' wealth and success to the Mets' is like comparing Randy Johnson to Eddie Gaedel. And that will always be the case, no matter how many Piazzas, Pedros, or Beltrans the Mets sign.

Even with Axis One—more money than God—firmly in place, the Evil Empire of the Yankees could not stand upright. No, evil needs to seek out more evil to survive, just like J.Lo seeks out new husbands. So, just as the Yankees had started to enjoy the lucrative benefits of being the only team in New York (no offense to Mets fans), a few years later a man took over the helm of this megalithic money ship, whose moral character is, shall we say, more than a bit shaky. Enter Axis of Baseball Evil #2, George Steinbrenner.

> **JOSH:** I can't stand Yankee fans who say they love the team but disapprove of Steinbrenner. It just doesn't make any sense.
> **KEVIN:** Makes sense to me. You can love your country but still not approve of its leadership.

JOSH: Are you suggesting that Steinbrenner should be impeached?
KEVIN: A capital idea.

Steinbrenner's obsessive-compulsive desire for victory at any cost with no regard for the rules of decency or fair play is not all that unusual for the Yankees. Steinbrenner is perhaps a more contemporary and egregious example, but any team that wins with the frequency of the Yankees has had its share of driven leaders. For example: Yankee owner Jacob Ruppert bought Babe Ruth, Waite Hoyte, Harry Harper, Wally Schang Mike McNally, and manager Ed Barrow all from the Red Sox, all after the 1919 season ended. He bought many more Red Sox players in the next three years to build his dynasty. After a lopsided trade between the Sox and Yankees in 1922, the St. Louis Browns complained that the Yanks were buying up all of the top talent. Commissioner Kennesaw Mountain Landis ruled that from then on, no trades could be made after June 15, except for those that cleared waivers.

> In a tough age which called for tough men in baseball, the Yankees were the toughest. They were managed by a perfectionist, bossed by a president who hated second place, and owned by a man who could say, even with a seventeen-game lead in 1936, "I can't stand the suspense. When are we going to clinch it?"
>
> **—David Voigt in *American Baseball***

Prior to Steinbrenner, the Yankees had a slightly different way to win championships. In a seemingly opposite strategy, the Yanks were famous for underpaying players. How could this work, one might ask? Because they still had the biggest flow of cash generated from being in the biggest market. The Yanks built their empire in a time when free agency wasn't allowed, and owners literally walked all over most of their players, even their stars. Yankee owners had enough cash flow to win championships and line their own coffers, rather than cut their players in on any of the take.

In selling the team to CBS Broadcasting, who in turn sold the Yankees to Steinbrenner, the Yankees organization in effect sold its collective soul to a man who would indiscriminately spend the mountain of cash that the Yankees had always been sitting on. Good for the Yankees, but bad for baseball. And it has reached catastrophic proportions, as the Yankees' payroll for 2005 exceeds the aggregate total of the bottom five teams' payrolls.

In today's environment, a financially conservative owner is crippling to a team's ability to win, primarily because of the environment that Steinbrenner's spending tactics have created. Player salaries are driven sky high to the point that the wealthier teams must spend more and more just to try to keep pace, and the poorer teams are forced to rid their payrolls of their marquee players just as they are starting to mature. Just ask the Oakland A's who traded away two of their big three pitchers between the 2004 and 2005 seasons.

Stein goes after high-priced free agents like Britney Spears goes after rednecks. And while this behavior is legal within the rules, it decimates any hope of competitive balance in the game. And Stein couldn't care less, as long as the Yankees win.

In this sense, Steinbrenner perfectly fits the ethos that the Yankees organization had begun adopting and, in turn, force-feeding to the baseball world even before his arrival. Note to Yankees fans: Force-feeding invokes hatred, it's a simple fact.

Due to George's many errors in judgment and many rule violations, the Yankees and Major League Baseball have had plenty of opportunities to rid themselves of him forever. Yet Steinbrenner has persevered. And worse, Steinbrenner has been allowed to help shape the rules that allow for the continuation of such excesses. It's how he has ensured his winning ways.

Why should we expect anything different from baseball in the age of corporate greed and conglomeration? Steinbrenner has exemplified the values of the 1980s and continues the tradition right alongside executive thieves like those at Enron, Tyco, and World-Com. Lose your butt in the tech-bust? Blame Steinbrenner, we say.

Steinbrenner does have his apologists who claim that he is a great owner because he's been willing to spend his own money—up against the Turners, Disneys, and other big corporations that have owned other teams. But this sorry argument holds no water. Certainly George is motivated by winning, and perhaps little else. But winning World Championships is synonymous with making money. When the Yankees win a World Series, George sees an enormous return on any money of his own that he invests. It's the way of business, and since baseball has become big business, it's more and more the way of baseball. Every Yankee championship lines Steinbrenner's pockets first and foremost.

But even so, Stein could not complete his dominance over the game without the Third Axis of Baseball Evil. Even with all the money in the world and a man who would seemingly sell his grandmother if there were an extra nickel in it for him, the teepee still couldn't stand on two legs alone. There would still be the problem of talent. Other teams might have talented scouts who could find talented young players and develop them with good coaching within their systems and find ways to defeat all that Yankee money in the end.

> When I covered the Yankees in the '60s, they had players like Horace Clarke, Ross Moschitto, Jake Gibbs, and Dooley Womack. It was like the first-team missed the bus.
>
> —Joe Garagiola

So, how does a business-minded capitalist eliminate the possibility of all competition? Simple: Since the Yankees have (by far) the most of a particular commodity (income), for them to win more consistently they had to eliminate the talent and skill components and turn baseball into a purely money-driven game. Then, the team with the most money (the Yankees) would always win, or at least have such an overwhelming advantage that they would always be close. But how can baseball be made into a game based more purely on money?

The answer to this conundrum came in the form of unrestricted free agency in a league without a team salary cap. Free agency is the Third Axis of Baseball Evil. Is it any coincidence that the Steinbrenner Yankees won their first World Series in 1978 just two years after the advent of free agency? And they did it with two key players—Reggie Jackson and Catfish Hunter—who they had lured away with bigger salary offers from an Oakland A's dynasty that had won three World Series in a row. We think not. Championship bought and paid for—and ever since then it has only gotten worse. How many Yankees on the current roster came up through the system? You can count them on one hand. Compare this number to the number of high-priced free agents on the Milwaukee Brewers. Did you come up with the same number?

Under this type of system, the teams from the big-moneyed markets will always get the best of the free-agent crop. The Yankees usually offer the most money, and even when they don't are always in the mix for any marquee player. Therefore, they either get the best of the best players available, or drive the price up for other teams.

I don't know if I want to go to New York. They'll have to pay me a lot more money because I like it here in Kansas City.

—Roger Maris

Now, from the players' perspective, the world prior to free agency was one of veritable indentured servitude to one team and one owner's whims and desires. This was certainly not a fair system. Thus, free agency resulted, as a matter of course, allowing players the freedom to move to the team that would pay them the highest possible salary, after a reasonable period of paying their dues to the team that signed them originally. And who wouldn't want a system like this? It's the free market. It's America. No one's telling Ben Affleck *that he must work with a particular studio* and that he can only make $10 million per movie, right? So why should it be different with baseball players?

Well, it's not any different at all. When a studio pays too much for a high-ticket actor, it must then cut costs in other areas in order to afford the big star. This translates to getting a cheaper cinematographer, bad writers, and crummy supporting actors. What do you get with this recipe? Movies like *Gigli* and *Daredevil*. Or to use Kevin Costner as an example, movies like *Waterworld* and *The Bodyguard*. Bad movies. Horrible movies. Movies people don't want to sit through.

JOSH: Ben is a huge Red Sox fan and a Yankee-hater, and I respect him for that.
KEVIN: Do you think *Gigli* is a good film?
JOSH: I blame J.Lo. She's from the Bronx.

The truth is, when we watch the Yankees win the American League's Eastern Division eight times in a row, we feel like we're trapped in a bad movie. The doors are locked, we're strapped down to the seats, and a Ben Affleck movie marathon is on endless loop. Oh yeah, and the theater's on fire. And the worst thing is that many ballplayers in the game don't ever recall a time before free agency. They feel entitled to get all the money that's coming to them. It's sad, really, and it's ruining baseball.

> They [today's multimillionaire ballplayers] don't know who I was or that I played baseball.
>
> —Jim "Catfish" Hunter

This is why baseball needs a hard salary cap: to bring the obscene spending under control and inject a much-needed dose of common sense back into the game. Under a salary cap, Kansas City still wouldn't be on a level playing field with New York, because New York would likely still outspend the Royals. But with talented scouts, coaches, players, and maybe a bit of luck, the Royals might have the chance to get into the playoffs once every decade or so. As it stands now, the Royals and the bottom third of teams in market size are out of contention by mid-June. And while every few years one of the middle-third franchises on the payroll scale may make the playoffs, they have little chance to win the World Series. It's just as the Yankees want it: competition eliminated.

This system isn't *baseball*, it's *money ball*. And it goes against the very idea of the American Dream that this country was founded on. Baseball fans are starting to ask themselves the sobering question: "What point is there to watching baseball when only the top salaried teams have any chance of winning?" And they're absolutely correct in asking this question. There is no point. If the little guy, through hard work and skill, cannot compete, then the American Dream is dead. And this is a baseball world and an America that we do not want to live in.

And while the players' union will fight a salary cap to the death, in the end, if a cap is not instituted, baseball will slide further into insignificance, and baseball will become that bad movie, predictable, and with the same tired script repeating itself season after season. Sort of the MLB equivalent of *Police Academy: Mission to Moscow*.

KEVIN: *Leonard: Part VI* was like watching *Yankee Dynasty: Part VI*.
JOSH: How about *Battlefield Earth* as *Battlefield Yankee*. Ouch.

We don't want this, baseball doesn't want this, and neither do you. But this is precisely what is happening to the game we all love. This Axis of Baseball Evil is not only what is wrong with the Yankees, it's what is wrong with the game as a whole. The theater is on fire, we're strapped into our seats, and *Ishtar* is beginning for the third time.

> **The door would be opened wide to the buying of success by the more affluent clubs, public suspicion would be aroused, traditional and sound methods of player development and acquisition would be undermined, and our efforts to preserve competitive balance would be greatly impaired.**
>
> **—Commissioner Bowie Kuhn, after voiding the sale of Joe Rudi, Rollie Fingers, and Vida Blue for cash by the World Champion Oakland A's**

So, while we understand that the game has obviously changed since free agency came about, it was something that needed to happen. But unrestricted free agency without a team salary cap is a recipe that will perpetuate a system that keeps the richest teams forever on top and the poorest teams forever on the bottom. It's grotesquely un-American.

What we are really advocating is for the return of the talents of scouting, coaching, and the developing of players to become meaningful to the game again. Because as it stands now, the best players will always be Yankees (or Red Sox, Angels, or Dodgers) in the end. And the movie will never change.

And if New Yorkers want to do something about the other two Axes of Baseball Evil, God love 'em for it. If they want to welcome another team into New York to divide Big Stein's profits, we're all for it. And if they want to rid themselves of King George altogether, we'll help plot the revolution.

Never is a concept the Yankees won't
ever come across.
—Andy Pettitte

Chapter Twelve

The Yankees Always Get You in the End

Kevin here again, with another true tale of the intersection of baseball and my family. They go hand in hand for me. For some reason, they always have.

The fall of 1995 saw the very worst and the very greatest of happenings in my life—all coming down simultaneously, of course. Why is it that while some of your dreams are coming true, other realities in life crash down around you?

In September of '95, I started getting postcards from friends from all over the country with statements written on them like, "What's up with the Mariners?" I had to laugh at each note that I got, because my M's (a veritable farm team for the rest of the league for nearly two decades) were pulling off one of the greatest pennant comebacks in baseball history. On August 24, the M's were 11½ games behind the AL West leading Anaheim/LA/California Angels. They were Anaheim at the time . . . God knows what name they're going by these days. And remember, it was Mariner Mario Mendoza about whom the phrase "the Mendoza line" was coined. As if we needed further proof that the team had always been an embarrassment prior to this year.

But these were the Mariners of Edgar and Tino Martinez, Randy Johnson, Ken Griffey, Jr., and Jay Buhner. Led by former Yankee Lou Piniella, these were the guys for whom the saying "Refuse to Lose" came to be, and in battling for the AL Wildcard spot, they managed to exceed all expectations and actually tie the AL West–leading Angels in the standings by finishing with an identical 78–66 record, thus forcing a one-game playoff. And in a final twist of fate, the playoff game was to be played in Seattle, pitting M's ace Randy Johnson against former Mariner (and the best pitcher the M's had ever had prior to Johnson) Mark Langston, who they had traded away to Montreal to acquire the "Big Unit" in the first place.

And, as if the drama needed any heightening, because the Yankees finished with a record of 79–65, the Bronx Bombers had the Wildcard sewn up. The winner of the one-game playoff would finish 79–66 and win the division, while the loser would drop to 78–67 and fall just one game short of the playoffs. It was winner take all.

It should have been the happiest day of my life. After all, I'd only been dreaming about the Mariners making the playoffs for twenty long seasons. And it was as if the planets were aligning, at long last, and my greatest baseball wish was being granted.

But I watched that one-game playoff from a hospital room, sitting beside my very ill grandmother. My mom's mom was not really a baseball fan, but she didn't like bullies either. And even this sickly woman who'd never sat through an entire baseball game in her life knew the Yankees to be precisely that. Before the game started, she said to me, "I hope your team wins," then she nodded off to sleep.

She'd been in the hospital for weeks, being treated for stomach cancer. As she slept, I watched the game. It was tense, and I held her hand. As the Mariners put a whooping on the Angels, I felt her squeeze my hand back ever so slightly.

All of baseball seemed to be rooting for the Mariners. Their run from perennial goats to heroes played an enormous role in bringing back to the game fans that were still angry, and rightly so, after the 1994 World Series had been cancelled because of the work stoppage. Seattle was transformed into a baseball town overnight. Popular support for a new ballpark reached an all-time high, just in time for the vote. And exactly two hours after the game ended, my grandmother died.

The events surrounding her funeral were interspersed with family members huddled around televisions to watch the Mariners ALDS against the Yankees. While our minds were on the death of our beloved family matriarch, the game provided a much needed distraction from our grief. It gave our family something else to talk about. Baseball can have that effect on grieving families.

But the death of my grandmother, who was a very faith-filled woman and who we all knew would have considerable pull in the afterlife with God, had done little to help the Mariners in their first playoff series. The Yankees had taken a 2–0 series lead in the Bronx, with Jim Leyritz providing a great deal more pop for the Yanks than was his due. Was it too much to ask for our grieving family to have the Mariners slip by the dreaded Yankees? Things looked bleak, indeed. It seemed our family could not defeat death, and we could not defeat the Yankees.

My grandmother was buried on the day the teams traveled back to Seattle, and somehow, after her body had been consecrated and given back to the earth, everything changed. The upstart M's, playing with nothing to lose, came home to win Game 3, breathing a much needed bit of life into the city. But there were still two more games ahead of them, a seemingly impossible hill to climb—especially against the Yankees.

But the Yankees didn't count on my grandmother, and they didn't count on Edgar Martinez. In the bottom of the eigth inning of Game 4, with the game knotted at six a piece and the dominant John Wetteland on the mound for the Yankees, Edgar Martinez crushed a grand slam off a 2–2 pitch that put the M's up for good. The entire city of Seattle erupted at once. There was new life, new hope, and a chance. The Kingdome echoed with chants of "Refuse to Lose!" and "Yankee Go Home!" Edgar had us rolling, and we knew it.

Game 5 was no less dramatic. Tied at four after nine innings, the Mariners brought in their dominant lefthander, Randy Johnson, to pitch in relief. The score remained tied through the tenth, but the Yankees pulled off a miracle of their own and scored a run in the top of the eleventh to take a 5–4 lead. "Black" Jack McDowell was on the mound for the Yanks in the bottom half. With Joey Cora and Griffey on base, Edgar stepped up to the plate once again. I had prayed harder for my grandmother to stay alive, but I was certainly imploring God, my grandmother, and all the saints to give Edgar the chance to do what he always seemed able to do. My prayer was answered.

Edgar responded by launching a rocket-fueled double that scored both base runners to win the game and capture the series. The M's had accomplished the unthinkable. The city streets stayed crowded late into the night with folks drinking and dancing and strangers high-fiving and hugging each other. It was a release of purest joy after eighteen seasons of angst. Edgar had hit .571 for the series and driven in ten runs. The press called him the "Yankee Killer with a Golden Bat." Edgar had been all that and more. It was a glorious time for M's fans.

So great was our love for Edgar, he had earned the status of honorary family member. After all, in our minds, our grandmother and he had inspired it all. She'd talked it over with God and made the Big Guy upstairs see things our way, and God had responded by allowing playoff Edgar to be even better than regular-season Edgar—which was no small feat. Together, she and Edgar had helped the M's to vanquish the Yankees in three straight games. Because the Mariners had bested the Yankees, we knew that somehow our grandmother must have been involved and had therefore bested death. There was no other possible explanation. And even though the M's lost to the Indians in the ALCS, it didn't matter. Not to us. We had slain the hydra. We had beaten the Yankees, damn it. We had beaten the New York Yankees in the playoffs. It was a joy few teams would ever know.

But apparently, George Steinbrenner didn't take too kindly to our grandmother's interference in his affairs. After a loud and obnoxious post-playoff-loss tantrum, he redoubled his efforts, and in the off-season acquired our Tino Martinez, Jeff Nelson, and even the bad-ball hitting Luis Sojo. In doing so, he began the crumbling of a dynasty that might have been. (He later also wound up with both Alex Rodriguez and Randy Johnson in his clutches, future Hall of Famers and crucial members of the Mariner dynasty that never was to be.)

And most disturbing of all, the Yankees have pummeled the Mariners in the playoffs ever since. We hadn't slain the hydra, because hydras have ten heads. We'd only managed to chop off one of them. And the other nine have come back to bite us again and again.

The 2000 playoffs pitted Seattle in its first ever ALCS against the Yankees. But there was unfinished business on the part of the Yanks. The M's fought bravely, but the Yankees remembered their defeat of 1995. They remembered it too well, spanking the Mariners four games to two.

The Mariners had been hemorrhaging Hall of Famers the way Ashlee Simpson lost fans after her "vocal malfunction" debacle on *Saturday Night Live*: Randy Johnson, Ken Griffey, Jr., and A-Rod had bolted in three successive seasons. It was a series of crushing blows that would have destroyed any franchise (other than the Yankees, of course). At least we never lost Edgar, reaffirming my belief that *there are* some things in this life that are untainted.

But during the miracle Mariner season of 2001, the M's won 116 games, more than any team in AL history, and they did it without these future Hall of Famers. Still led by Lou Piniella, the great Edgar, and Ichiro, the M's seemed destined to make it to their first World Series. But at the end of the long road, there stood the Yankees, again waiting to put another smack-down on the Seattle Mariners, still angry and spiteful for the humiliation of 1995.

It would be foolish for our family to believe that our grandmother's influence could have held on forever. But Steinbrenner and his Yankees are the forces of darkness for our family (at least my mother's side). We may have been able to avoid the pain that the dark specter of Steinbrenner was to put down on our family, and our ball club, but someday everyone must answer to the Yankees.

Chapter Thirteen

The Yankee Mystique—
The Mystery Unraveled

The essence of the Yankees is that they win. From in front or from behind, they win. And that's why the history of the New York Yankees is virtually the history of baseball.

—Dave Anderson, *New York Times*

It's time for us and all of our Yankee-hating brethren to take a bit of a reality break. As difficult as it may be to admit, we must face the truth. We hate the Yankees because they win. Sure, there are other factors. But if the Yankees didn't win, there would be little about them to hate. Say it out loud once with us: "WE HATE THE YANKEES BECAUSE THEY WIN." Now breathe. There. That feels better, doesn't it?

> You kind of took it for granted around the Yankees that there was always going to be baseball in October.
> —Whitey Ford

What is it about those sons-a-guns, the New York Yankees? They have somehow captured and bottled that genie that everyone else in professional sports wants: continual success, year in and year out. It stinks, doesn't it? And the rest of us—from Boston to San Diego, from Seattle to Miami, and from Cleveland to Texas—loathe them for it, one and all.

Fans of the Yanks answer the unified front of combined hatred offered them by the rest of the nation with these words: "It's because we're winners. People love us and hate us for the same reason—because we win baseball games." While it is undoubtedly true that over the years the Yankees have built baseball's Iron Giant, this deluded viewpoint of their fans hopelessly over-simplifies the issue. The Yankees don't merely build dynasties—their dynasties are handed down from one generation to the next. Yankee teams that do not win championships, and preferably back-to-back dynastic reigns of utter and total domination, well, they get into trouble quick in Yankeetown, USA. Over their history of championships, winning has evolved for the Yankees from lucky happenstance to the building of dynasties, then devolved into an exercise in dominance, to bored expectation, to an obsessive compulsion. And through this devolution, the Yankees have become the most supported, and conversely most hated, franchise in the history of sports. The legions of Yankee-hater nation are swelling every year, and might be the single biggest group of sports fans in the country—next to Yankee fans, that is.

For a better understanding of this phenomenon, let's take a look at a few of the more prolific dynasties in sports history. As of 2005, the Montreal Canadians had won twenty-four Stanley Cups since their inception in 1909. The Boston Celtics had more NBA titles than any other team—an impressive sixteen, including a span of nine in a row at one stretch. The UCLA Bruins had won eleven NCAA men's basketball titles, including a dominant run that included seven straight titles between the years of 1967–1973. This feat, perhaps, stands out among any that we can conceive of, as least likely to ever be duplicated in the history of sports.

But there seems to be little hatred reserved for these dynasties. Sure, one could argue that winning twenty-four Stanley Cups is a more dominant feat than winning twenty-six (or more) World Series, what with the grueling physical punishment a team must endure throughout hockey's unending season and brutal multitiered playoffs.

And take the UCLA Bruins winning all those titles under head coach John Wooden. Many fans and foes alike look to those as the halcyon years of college hoops. Sure there are UCLA Bruin-haters out there aplenty, but nothing like the venomous legions spawned by the Yankees. Most fans of college basketball respect John Wooden and the great UCLA Bruins' tradition that he built with his teams. Kevin is a Gonzaga University graduate, and although he hopes that his Zags beat UCLA by twenty points every time they play, there is far less loathing and focus upon that one storied franchise than there is with the Yanks. Josh likewise laments the fact that Lew Alcindor chose to attend UCLA after a recruiting visit to his alma mater, the College of the Holy Cross, but he still respects the Bruins' tradition, while he feels nothing but contempt for everything Yankee.

So we had to wonder, just why this is the case? Why have other teams with dominant dynasties not been so reviled and disliked, both within their own sport and globally? After all, does anyone inside or outside the NHL hate Les Canadiens with every fiber of their being? Can you find passionate Detroit Red Wings fans or Boston Bruins fans who so despise the top dog Habs that they dedicate their lives to their destruction? Perhaps, but it is admittedly much more difficult to muster extreme hate for the Canadians in general. None of these passionate rivalries inspire Yankee levels of hatred.

Likewise, the Celtics do not inspire a national front of hatred like the Yanks do. Certainly, there are circles of intensity, such as in LA and Detroit, for those who remember the epic battles of the 1980s. But those Celtic, Laker, and Piston fans also look to those years as the glory years of the NBA. Although there is intense dislike, there is also mutual respect and even a friendly sense of one-upmanship and friendly rivalry between competitors. They considered one another worthy adversaries.

Yankee hatred is so pervasive that when we unofficially polled countries in the Balkans who have been in a blood-feud with one another for thousands of years, even they agreed that no one among them wants to see the Yanks win another one in October.

Why, then, is it so easy to hate the Yankees with such unbridled passion, with such utter contempt and vigor? We can answer with three words: The Yankee Mystique.

You don't have to look too hard to find it. The image of the Yankees we are force-fed through the media tells us all what we never needed to know: that they are clean-cut boys who win because they're more talented than all other players, live right, and abide by all the rules of fair play. The Yankees are a first rate, first-class act all down the line. They deserve the best of everything (which is exactly what they get), and because they are provided the best, in return they produce the one thing their fans want: wins, wins, and more wins. Further, we are told, the Yankees deserve all these wins because they go about their business in the right way: the American way. They are hardworking, honest American boys who win because, darn it, they just want it more, they try harder, and they live right. And thus, God has made life more difficult on Yankee opponents.

To this we say: "Spare us this tripe!" Nothing could be further from the truth. And this Yankee Yammering is what makes fans of all other teams, other sports, even other nations, hate the Yankees more than any other mortal enemies that have ruled roughshod over the earth.

Undoubtedly, the Yanks win. They win because they have the best players. They have the best players because they have the most money. And they have the most money because they win and therefore have the largest and most loyal fan base. You see what a snowball effect this has had? Only the big bang had more momentum.

And so the ever-present and growing Yankee Mystique is enough to kill the will of most other teams by Opening Day.

Just what is all this hullabaloo about Yankee Mystique, and from whence did it come? Are the Yankees truly divinely blessed, as their fans and management as well as the media would have us believe? It would certainly seem to be so, as many of their foes can attest, having gone down in flames underneath the Yankee Juggernaut, even after building up seemingly insurmountable leads over the Bronx Bombers.

Or, rather, is the Yankee Mystique some sort of self-fulfilling prophecy? Have the combined forces of baseball legions been summarily hoodwinked by this so-called "mystique"? Do normally sane and rational umpires favor Yankee players, perhaps even on a subconscious level, because of this phenomenon? Do teams that have sound fundamentals and have played so well in the regular season simply choke when facing the Yanks in October because they feel somehow less worthy of victory? And do mediocre players somehow manage to play great ball once they put on a Yankee uniform?

The secret of success in pitching lies in getting a job with the Yankees.
—Waite Hoyt

Sadly, the answer to all of these questions (and we're not the least bit proud to admit this) is yes.

Perhaps the most glaring example of the Yankee Mystique in action was the 1978 season. On July 19 the Yankees trailed Boston in the American League East standings by fourteen games. It seemed all but sewn up for the Sox. However, a cataclysmic freefall combined with a Yankee surge put the Yankees on top of the standings with just a few games left in the season.

After dropping six straight games to the Yanks late in the season, the Spaceman, Sox pitcher Bill Lee, said:

Our pain isn't as bad as you might think. Dead people don't suffer.

—Bill Lee

But then a miracle occurred. The Sox woke from their slumber and managed to win their last eight games to wind up tied with the Yankees atop the standings—both clubs finishing the season with a record of 99–63. A one-game playoff was scheduled at Fenway to decide which team would be the AL East division champs.

On that fateful day, Boston etched out 2–0 lead through six innings, on an RBI single by Jim Rice and a Carl Yastrzemski dinger off of Yankee ace Ron Guidry. But the Yanks put two on in the top of the seventh and brought their weak hitting shortstop, Earl Russell Dent, to the plate. And the rest, as they say, is history. Or mystery, if you prefer.

Anyone who follows baseball has seen the replay a hundred times of "Bucky" Dent's home run floating impossibly over the Green Monster like a butterfly trying to lift and anvil. It's continually voted one of the most dramatic and unlikeliest of home runs in baseball history and was enough to give the Yankees the win and launch them in dramatic fashion toward their inevitable World Series victory over the Dodgers.

Now if this isn't an example of Yankee Mystique—a very mediocre player coming up big in a clutch situation for the Yanks—we don't want to hear about what is. Consider that Dent only hit forty home runs in his entire career in more than 4,500 at bats. Certainly Don Zimmer (the Sox manager at the time) was considering his stats when he gave Dent the nickname "Bucky '*Bleeping*' Dent," or something along those lines. And Yankee fans of this era look to Dent's dinger as the prime example of just how much better players play when they don Yankee pinstripes. Obviously, God favors the Yankees (or so Yankee fans would have us believe).

It is precisely at times like these when the true character of the modern Yankee reveals itself. After the loss of the one-game playoff in 1978, one of many that the Sox endured during their eighty-six-year drought between World Series championships, one Yankee responded with:

I don't feel sorry for them—I pity them.

—Graig Nettles, Yankees third baseman, on the Red Sox

Ah, there's nothing like winning with class, is there? The Yankees had no doubt changed from a team that won with class and dignity to a team that not only expected to win, but derided the losing team. Continuing today, the so-called Yankee Mystique that propels the Yanks toward victory every season has sunk to the ugly attitude of feeling entitled to win. And so, the question begs, what lengths will the Yankees go to in order to protect their Mystique from decay?

Perhaps the answer to that question lies in the other side to the Bucky Dent story. There has been much speculation since that home run that Dent's bat was corked and his mystical dinger was, therefore, bogus. Dent has admitted that he had never previously used the bat in question that stroked the winning shot. We do know for certain that Mickey Rivers noticed that Dent's bat was cracked (from the dugout he spotted a hairline crack that Dent and the umpire could not see) and that Rivers loaned Bucky a bat, the bat with which he hit the home run. Rivers has publicly denied rumors that the loaner was corked, filled with superballs, a fungo, or in any other way enhanced.

Boston fans feel they were cheated. Yankee fans think all this talk is sour grapes from the Boston camp. Let's explore the facts. Here's Dent's hitting line for 1978. (These stats include the one-game playoff.)

G	AB	R	H	2B	3B	HR	RBI	BB
123	379	40	92	11	1	5	40	23

IBB	SO	SH	SG	HSP	GIDP	AVG	OBP	SLG
1	24	6	5	2	10	.243	.286	.317

Not very impressive, even in the weak hitting 1970s. Perhaps the most glaring statistic is that Dent only hit five balls out of any yard in 379 at bats in all of '78. For our math, that's one home run for every seventy-five at bats. And if you extend this thinking over Dent's entire career (forty home runs in 4,512 at bats), Bucky's homer is literally a one-in-a-hundred shot—actually one in more than a hundred. Yanks fans say this is what gives the homer its mystique, right? The average guy comes up big. The least likely of heroes rises at the necessary time. This is what Yankee greats do and what the Yankee Mystique mythology thrives on.

In actuality, Dent's five home runs in 1978 added up to a banner year for the diminutive hitter. Only five times in his twelve-year career did he hit five or more dingers in a season, and never once did Bucky hit as many as nine during a one-year span. Dent did go on to win MVP honors in the Yankees' World Series win over the Dodgers, poking out ten hits in twenty-four at bats for a .417 average—not bad for a guy who never even sniffed a .300 season in the bigs. (Perhaps he kept using Rivers' "lucky" bat in the series?)

In any case, Dent's home run will forever go down in Yankee folklore as a return to glory for the Yankees. We're just glad that the Yanks couldn't pull out another World Series victory for another eighteen seasons after that. And yes, those were the happiest eighteen years of our lives.

My only feeling for the Yankees is that I hate them.

—Rick Burleson, Red Sox SS, after the one-game playoff   135

While we may never be certain that Dent (and/or Rivers) cheated that fateful day, October 2, 1978, it does seem a bit curious in retrospect that he never hit as well during any other period in his career—we're betting clear back to his T-ball days in Savannah, Georgia, although, admittedly, we have not checked that far back. As for Rivers, this is a guy who once said:

George [Steinbrenner], Billy [Martin], and I—we're two of a kind.

—Mickey Rivers

We think that Rivers' own comparison of himself to Steinbrenner and Martin and his inability to count to three pretty much say it all.

It's Yankee mythmaking all over again. While the Bronx Bombers would like us to believe in their mystique—that they have a God-given priority to win ball games and their successes on the field are brought about by fair play—we don't buy it. In Ruth, Gehrig, DiMaggio, even Mantle, the Yankees had superior players and men of class. Players who could be looked up to as heroes by kids, both for their on-field excellence and for their public demeanor outside the lines. Well, not Mantle. Jim Bouton reveals him as a drunkard and a Peeping Tom in his book *Ball Four*. Ruth, although kind to children and likeable, was also a drunkard and a womanizer, and, if you believe the recent unauthorized biography, DiMaggio comes off as quite a bastard and a miser, but at least there's Gehrig.

We wonder if today's Yankee players even know who these men were. As George Michael (the sports guy, not the singer) used to say on his program *The Sports Machine* (long before the days of ESPN), "Let's go to the video tape." Even "Donnie Baseball" admits having a bit of trouble with the Yankee Mystique.

> Honestly, at one time I thought Babe Ruth was a cartoon character. I really did, I mean, I wasn't born until 1961, and I grew up in Indiana.
>
> **—Don Mattingly**

Take courage, Donnie. There's always time to catch up on your baseball history.

And what of the other "magical moments" in Yankee history that are questionable in retrospect? In the 2001 ALDS Derek Jeter performed what is now known only as "the play." Jeter relayed a dribbling throw from right fielder Shane Spencer and flipped it home to get out a sluggish Jeremy Giambi, who was chugging in so slowly from third base he was like a turtle with a bum leg and a belly full of steroids. The press claims Jeter's heads-up play saved the game and the series for the Yanks. The truth is, however, that Jeter did nothing more than was required of him. Backing up the cutoff man is his role in that situation.

> **KEVIN:** Since when is doing something you're supposed to "heads up?"
> **JOSH:** When you have the Yankee press engine following your every move.
> **KEVIN:** It's another Giambi fiasco.

It was merely dumb luck, and nothing more, that Giambi was chugging around the base paths slower than an arthritic octogenarian and that he hadn't crossed the plate days earlier. Even a player of half-decent speed would have turned "the play" into "the too little, too late, fairly effeminate backhand toss." Does it sound like sour grapes that we blame Giambi rather than give Jeter credit? Well, it's the truth, and somebody should be saying so.

Now, let's make one thing crystal clear. We do not advocate measures that would eradicate the dynastic franchises. Sure, more competitive balance would be a good thing, so that teams like the Pirates and the Royals are not out of contention by mid-May each season. But the last thing that Major League Baseball needs is the rotating champions system that now exists in the NBA. We may never see an NBA team dominate the way the Celtics did in the 1960s, the Celts and the Lakers did of the 1980s, or the Bulls in the 1990s. And really, what fun is it not to have that dark specter of the evil-that-be overcome? It's the stuff of every great heroic tale in history.

Whether it's the Marlins of 2003 or the Diamondbacks of 2001, has there been anything more exciting in sports to watch than the bulked-up Yankees of New York getting knocked off by teams with a fraction of their payroll? It's fun to see those camera shots of Steinbrenner smoking and fuming way up high in the solitude of his luxury box as his payroll goes down the toilet against players with more desire that play together as a team.

But the Yankees attempt to use these examples of smaller-market teams making the World Series, and even winning championships over them, to bolster their argument of how baseball isn't broken at all and that money only matters in the game when it's used properly. We can only assume that by "proper" advocates for the current system mean that money is spent the way that the Yankees spend theirs.

Isn't this argument a bit like Norm, from the PBS television show *The New Yankee Workshop*, telling us that we too can build at home the very same quality oak hutch that's at the furniture store for a fraction of the cost (to display all our World Series trophies, no doubt) just as he built the one on the show? Never mind that Norm has use of half a million dollars in routers, table saws, band saws, sanders—all the tools that make the job doable at home in the first place. And let's face it: the Pittsburgh Pirates are putting some pretty ugly furniture on the field.

And let us not forget one significant—yet somehow underreported—fact about postseason revenues: Even though the Yankees lost to the Diamondbacks in the 2001 World Series, New York still received more playoff profits than did Arizona. According to *USA Today* and the *Baseball Prospectus*, the Yankees netted $16 million in playoff revenue during the 2001 postseason, while the world champion Diamondbacks garnered only $13 million. How can this be possible, you ask? When it comes to revenues, the Yankees get the largest slice of the pie, win, lose, or rain delay. It's as simple as that. Even when the Yankees lose, they still win.

Even though Florida and Arizona managed exciting victories over the Yanks in the World Series, the biggest stage baseball has, both teams fell back down to earth the very next season, alongside the A's, the Royals, and a dozen other teams that have little chance at a World Series appearance. At the Goliath end of the spectrum, the Yankees' money has all but guaranteed their playoff attendance year after year. Small-money teams have to be perfect all season long to reach the play-offs, while the Yankees have insulated themselves against having to be perfect. They need only to perform adequately to reach the postseason. They're so overloaded with talent, even their bench players should perform better than these small-market starters, because many of them are paid more to pinch hit every third game or so in New York than starters get in Tampa Bay. So this false Yankee argument holds little water.

Look at all the factors that could have upset the apple-cart of the 2003 Marlins on their quest toward the World Series: They could afford no stupid signings of overrated steroid-fueled free agents that crapped out midseason; they relied on excellent young and cheap pitching and position players that could not have flinched under their initial pennant race and playoff pressures; they could afford no injuries to key lineup players and no player scandals or other such club-house distractions; they relied on their low-rent veterans to have comeback years; and their wise and aged manager Jack McKeon not only had to remain healthy and alert throughout the playoffs, but the Marlins could not have afforded him to have had even one "senior moment" handling his pitching staff (see Boston manager Grady Little leaving Pedro Martinez on the mound too long that year in the ALCS as an example). Every single one of these factors and many others had to align in perfect unison for the Marlins to win that sole World Series. And any one of these factors not going precisely the way of the Marlins would likely have swung the balance back to the heavily favored and all-mighty Yankees.

On the other hand, look at the payroll-laden Yankees in 2005. Even after their pitching staff was decimated by injuries, they still had enough in the bank to gamble on Al Leiter in the middle of the season to help them amble their way toward the playoffs.

So which team's performance is most deserving of the "mystique" label: the team that has all the cards stacked in its favor or the team that had to be perfect? We suspect (as we hope you are beginning to as well) that so-called Yankee Mystique died a quick and unnoticed death sometime around the time they unceremoniously booted Babe Ruth out of the clubhouse, giving him the bum's rush, and that the Yankees have been coasting on fumes ever since.

The myth is that you put a Yankee uniform on a player and he becomes great.
—Manager Birdie Tebbetts

Chapter Fourteen

Into the Heart of Darkness

As baseball stadiums go, we both agree that Yankee Stadium is one of the most impressive. We can't deny that it is regal and historic, and endowed with the types of genuine quirks and nuisances that many of the newer ballparks lack. As far as atmosphere, though, Yankee Stadium is the most menacing big league park for visiting players and fans—and we don't believe baseball parks should ever be menacing. We believe they should be warm and inviting.

In researching our first book together, *The Ultimate Baseball Road Trip*, we traveled to all thirty major league stadiums. Most of baseball's parks and fans made us feel right at home. Even though we weren't always rooting for the home team, we usually settled into our seats and immediately made new friends who helped us understand the big picture of baseball from their perspective. Hot dogs were eaten, suds were sipped, baseball stories and tales from the road were

> When I was a little boy,
> I wanted to be a
> baseball player and join
> a circus. With the
> Yankees I've
> accomplished both.
> —Graig Nettles

exchanged, and a good time was had by all. That's the great thing about baseball. At ball yards across the country, fans sit elbow to elbow with one another and share the wonders of the game, paying no heed to distinctions of gender, age, ethnicity, social class, or politics. In these moments, the game can be a tremendous source of unity across this great land of ours. It allows fans of all shapes, sizes, creeds, and colors to identify with one another through a common passion, while leaving room for some people to root for the home team and others to root for the visitors.

Such is not the case at Yankee Stadium. In New York fans chant cruel epithets at visiting players (and sometimes at home players). They dump beverages on visiting players who dare to approach the outfield fences. They throw batteries and sometimes even portable radios at visiting players when they make nice plays. They throw trash and food onto the field when umpires make calls they don't like. They single out any nonconformist fans brazen enough to wear another team's colors and taunt and threaten them until they remove the "offensive garments." As the beer flows, this taunting often degenerates into physical violence. In sum, it's the Yankee Way or the Highway for fans of other teams. Where there should be unity, there is only conformity. Where there should be E. Pluribus Unum, there is only Yankee mind control.

JOSH: I can't sit here if I'm going to wear a Portland Seadogs hat.
KEVIN: Sure you can! This is still America, isn't it?

JOSH: But that six-year-old girl just flipped me off.
KEVIN: Yeah, and her mom did too.

The situation has gotten so bad that even the Yankees themselves realize they can no longer control their own fans. Beer is no longer sold in the bleacher sections of Yankee Stadium. We say, a baseball team deciding not to sell beer to thirsty fans is like a movie theater deciding not to sell popcorn. Usually bleacher seats are the cheapest in the park, so the teams make up the difference by selling overpriced drafts to the bleacher creatures. It's the American way . . . or at least one small wrinkle of the American ballpark experience. But not in New York, where the Yankees must have finally realized the extra security details and law suits were costing them more than they were making in beer sales.

KEVIN: So instead of getting rid of the idiots, they got rid of the beer? Incredible.
JOSH: And good-natured peace-loving seam-heads like us have to endure these idiots while we're stone-cold sober.

It is true that these types of unruly fan behaviors are becoming more common throughout the game as fans pay higher prices for tickets and concessions and come to expect more from the ballpark experience and from the home team. But Yankee Stadium has always been the industry leader in fan misconduct. This is the place where a fan once threw a four-inch hunting

Some yard.
—Babe Ruth, upon stepping onto the field at Yankee Stadium for the first time in 1923

knife out of the upper deck, hitting California first baseman Wally Joyner in the arm following an Angels' victory. This is where it became trendy for fans to send one of their drunken emissaries onto the field late in games to run circles around inept ballpark security guards. This is where a fan once jumped from the upper deck and spent an entire half inning suspended on the protective screen behind home plate while the game continued. That's right. They had to keep playing with the fan on the screen because they couldn't get him down and had no other choice. Like we said, they have completely lost control.

This is where armed police officers wearing riot gear had to surround the field to protect the players during Game 6 of the 2004 American League Championship Series after the umpires correctly ruled that Alex Rodriguez was out at first base because he had sissy-slapped the ball out of Bronson Arroyo's glove. When the initial ruling that proclaimed A-Rod safe was overturned, New York fans went ballistic, throwing all manner of debris on the field. And it's sadly typical of these fans. Yankee fans are so used to the umpires bailing their team out of jams that they don't know how to react when the men in blue make the right call. This time there was no twelve-year-old fan to interfere with a deep fly ball and no bumbling second base umpire to say Chuck Knoblauch had registered a phantom force out. There was no bogus help of any kind. And so, the fans responded by becoming criminally belligerent, even though the replay on the stadium Jumbotron clearly showed that A-Rod had attempted to cheat.

The playoffs notwithstanding, there's no such thing as a friendly, relaxing day at the ballpark in this city. Even in mid-May, when the Yanks are playing the Devil Rays, have an eight game lead in the AL East, and are leading 6–0 in the third inning, tensions run high. This is baseball New York City–style—high expectations, high stress, and high crime. And no fun. Oh, and did we mention the high prices and high cholesterol levels at the concession stands?

JOSH: I'm putting my wallet in my front pants pocket just to be safe.

KEVIN: I'd do the same, but someone swiped mine three innings ago.

JOSH: That's terrible.

KEVIN: Not really. There was no cash in it. I spent my last $80 on the hot dog and beer run I made back in the fourth inning.

The Yankees and their fans are so obsessed with winning at all costs and with vanquishing their "enemies" that they have lost sight of the facts that every baseball game is a special occasion, whether or not the home team wins, and that every baseball fan shares a special bond with every other fan of the game. The poor lost souls who fill the House that Ruth Built can't just sit back and enjoy watching the innings unfold. Anticipation and concern over each game's end result override this simple pleasure. Fans are so preoccupied with whether or not the Yanks will win that they miss out on the beauty of the game's intricacies. And when things don't go the Yankees' way, rightly or wrongly, by hook or by crook, they turn their hostility toward the players and toward one another.

The Yankees organization does nothing to defuse this powder keg. Rather, in their infinite arrogance, the Yankee front office–types light the fuse. The team mythology celebrates its winning players and winning years to such a ludicrous extent that fans can't help but expect the Yankees to win every single game. The owner of the team also perpetuates a "football" mentality, often calling out the players and coaches in the media for minor lapses in play, even when those lapses occur early in the season or later in the season when the Yankees already have an insurmountable stranglehold on the division title.

From the moment fans step into Yankee Stadium, they are reminded that the Yankees are built to win. During batting practice, a highly self-celebratory Jumbotron presentation pays tribute to the Yankees' proud past. Clearly the Yankees are very proud of their past, because the show runs for a full hour, and after the first showing concludes, it starts up again right away . . . day after day, home stand after home stand, year after year. Rather than sitting and listening for the crack of the bat during BP, fans who arrive at the stadium without earplugs and blinders have no choice but to endure this ear-piercing, self-aggrandizing video indoctrination into Yankee fandom. We suspect, but cannot prove, that there are also subliminal messages embedded in the words and images that appear on the screen. All we know is that after watching for five minutes, Kevin ran to the souvenir stand and bought eight Derek Jeter bobble-head dolls. Don't worry, we later dismembered the dolls on our ride from New York to Philadelphia and littered the New Jersey Turnpike with little Derek Jeter arms and legs, much to the delight of other motorists.

The stadium's Monument Park, located behind the left field fence, is another popular attraction before games. We have to admit we can appreciate the history in this part of the stadium, but we do wonder if it is psychologically healthy for the Yankee fans and players to worship their demagogues in the same place where the team currently plays, rather than at a separate hall of fame location. If fans and players are constantly reminded of how great the Yankees' past was, how can the present team ever measure up? Yankee fans are conditioned to expect more of their team than it can possibly deliver.

Everything you hate about New York as a visitor, you love as a home player.
—Scott Brosius

All-time greats like Babe Ruth, Lou Gehrig, Joe DiMaggio, and Mickey Mantle only come along once in a franchise's history, if it's lucky. Yet there is a whole cast of superstars looming between the left field fence and bleachers in the form of statues and plaques. If that doesn't give fans

> Every day I went to the ballpark in Yankee Stadium as well as on the road, people were on my back. The last six years in the American League were mental hell for me. I was drained of all desire to play baseball.
> —Roger Maris

and players a superiority complex, we don't know what will. As a result, these fans often turn on their own players when they fail to live up to their ridiculously inflated expectations.

Our first trip to Yankee Stadium together featured the home team against the Baltimore Orioles in a meaningless game in late September. The Yankees had already clinched the American League East title, and the Orioles were going nowhere. The Yankees started Orlando Hernandez, who had just come off the disabled list, with the intention of seeing if he might be able to get his arm back in shape and give the team some quality innings in the postseason.

The game we saw was fairly uneventful. No one jumped out of the stands and ran onto the field, and we didn't observe any of the batteries that were thrown from the upper deck actually making contact with any of the Oriole players. The fans seated around us didn't go out of their way to befriend us, but they didn't harass us either—maybe that was because Josh sat with his Seadogs hat tucked in his pants and Kevin kept his brood of Derek Jeter dolls lined up like little soldiers guarding his seat.

The fans may have left us alone, but they did not enjoy their time at the ballpark. When Hernandez issued back-to-back walks early in the game, we overheard one fan seated near us ask another, "What the hell is Torre doing running this guy out there in the first place?" After a run-scoring single, another fan lamented, "They had Pettitte available on four-days rest." Soon a great many fans were booing Hernandez and calling, in no uncertain language, for Torre to take him out of the game. Mind you, Hernandez had won several big games for the team in previous postseasons and was rehabbing an injury. And Torre had guided the team to four World Series championships in the previous five years. But when total domination is promised, no substitute will do.

The fans weren't willing to grant Hernandez or Torre any leniency. They wanted Hernandez out of the game so that the Yankees would have the best chance of winning the game. Nothing else mattered to these so-called "best fans in baseball." It was as if they didn't realize or didn't care that the game was meaningless and that the entire point of the start was to let Hernandez get some innings under his belt so that he might be able to help the team win a game that actually mattered in October. When Torre finally yielded to the cat calls and went to the mound to take the ball, he was serenaded with boos, and then Hernandez got a Bronx Cheer as he trotted to the Yankee dugout.

Now, while we admit that all teams have a number of reactionary fans who have a limited knowledge of the game, only in New York would two men who had done so much for a franchise be booed for no good reason at all.

Like we said, so much for a relaxing day at the ballpark.

The biggest irony of all involving Yankee Stadium involves George Steinbrenner's relationship with the place. For almost three decades he hyped Yankee Stadium as the preeminent sporting venue on the planet, while he himself spent his summers in Tampa, watching the Yankees on satellite TV. But these days he isn't talking up the stadium at all because he wants the city to build a new stadium for the team in a "better" (read: cleaner, less dilapidated, more profit-producing) part of New York. And plans call for making the new Yankee Stadium more like the old ballpark before Steinbrenner and company had the place remodeled.

Certainly the current Yankee neighborhood deserves some attention in our discussion. Talk about ironies—one of the most arching symbols of American wealth and power is situated smack dab in the heart of one of New York's most derelict neighborhoods. The discrepancy between the haves and have-nots in our country is rarely as plain to see. While the Yankees are printing money as fast as they can inside the stadium, outside the neighborhood is sinking faster than a Randy Johnson splitter.

The most egregious example of all can be found in the youth baseball and soccer field that sits a few steps from the dive bars on River Avenue. This should be a wonderful place for the underprivileged kids of the Bronx to play ball in the shadows of Yankee Stadium. There's only one problem. The complex looks like it belongs in a third-world country. The grass is dead, there are craters in the infields and outfields and midfields, and the benches are broken and splintered. Right beside the most decadent baseball stadium in the U.S. sits one of the country's most pathetic and rundown youth complexes. It's disgraceful that this community has so little while the Yankees have so much. It's a shame that with all of the millionaire players

> They can't get any rougher on us unless they show up with Uzis.
> —Dave Justice, then playing for the Indians, before Game 6 of the 1998 ALCS

the Yankees have, not a single one has rectified this situation, if even to get the tax write-off that such a charitable act would provide.

Consider this: If Derek Jeter donated one game's salary (approximately $117,000) to revitalize the neighborhood, this complex could be transformed into a sparkling sports and entertainment center for the kids of the Bronx. Doubtless Jeter has driven past the place hundreds of times, but it still looks like a minefield rather than a ball field. For shame, Derek Jeter. A plague on all of your many houses. And on A-Rod's too.

Not surprisingly, the affluent white-collar Yankee fans hurry directly from their Mercedes and BMWs to the ballpark gates. These are the Heineken-sipping yuppies from midtown and Westchester who root for the Yankees from their box seats because the Yankees win, and each new notch on the team's World Series belt is a personal ego stroke for them. It would seem that because they are afraid or ashamed of the Bronx, they have trained themselves to look past it without even seeing it anymore. It's as if the crumbling buildings and desperate individuals who live in them don't even exist in their minds.

To ensure their fans avoid any unpleasantries, the Yankees have tried to make the entrance plaza between the stadium's main parking garage and ballpark gates a festive, friendly, shiny, safe place—a sort of substitute for a real ballpark neighborhood. Here, on the plaza, a Yankee fan can buy a hotdog and a soda, spending more money to do so than many families of four in the Bronx have to spend on food in a day. And as an added attraction, Yankee fans get to listen to the incessant incantations of the corporate marketers who pay the Yankees for floor space on the plaza. Who doesn't love to be harassed by credit card companies and life insurance hawks while heading into a ballgame? It's almost as much fun as fending off telemarketing calls during dinner. We say, "Well done, George. Well, done."

Yankee Stadium is extravagant, historic, and monumental. Unfortunately, the fans who fill it are beset by anxieties and unrealistic expectations. And to any non-brainwashed, objective visitor, the ironies of the Yankees' wealth are unsettling. As a result, the atmosphere does not allow much room for fans to appreciate the game's subtleties, lulls, and lighter moments. And that's a crying shame . . . and as Tom Hanks reminded us in *A League of Their Own*, there's not supposed to be any crying in baseball.

The best solution for overcrowding in New York would be to combine Nickel Beer Night with a baseball bat promotion at Yankee Stadium.
—Neil J. Liss

Chapter Fifteen

Yankee Imperialism

Without losers where would winners be?

—Casey Stengel

Perhaps every international traveler has a story such as this. When Kevin was traveling in London back in 1996, he was in a pub having a pint of Guinness while the rain pounded the dismal gray streets. He was dressed, very typically, as an American tourist: large backpack strapped over a Columbia rain jacket and baseball cap. A couple of college-aged kids sat down at the bar next to him, and one struck up a conversation.

"What team is that ya have on your hat there?" one asked.

"It's a Mariners cap," Kevin replied with pride.

"The Mariners? And just who in bloody hell are they?" the other chortled. As he took a long drink of his warm beer, Kevin thought to himself how difficult the young man's question was to answer.

"The Seattle Mariners," he said. "You follow baseball?"

"Football," said the first, and by this Kevin knew he was referring to soccer.

"The New York Yankees and that, right?" shouted the second, then dragged long and hard on his cigarette.

"Yeah," sighed Kevin, "the Yankees. You guys know any other teams?"

"Are there any other teams?" asked the first.

"Seattle's famous for music, right . . . Nirvana and Pearl Jam and that lot," stated the second plainly. Kevin nodded, not in agreement, but in recognition of these perceived truths. And he considered the fact that the Yankees hadn't won a World Series in more than seventeen years. What happened to the reputations of all these other teams?

Then, the first Brit made a shocking observation: "To us, you're all Yanks," he said, and Kevin wondered if he knew how profound the words he had just uttered were. Kevin bought a round of warm Tetley's for the kindly Limeys, and they all had a good laugh. These gents had been completely candid about what they knew. But incidents such as these have since taught us (both Josh and Kevin) a few lessons.

Obvious Lesson #1: The world knows that baseball is America's game and that the Yankees are the top (if only) dog.

Not as obvious Lesson #2: Not only do the Yankees symbolize America, but America has become symbolic of the Yankees.

For the rest of Kevin's trip through Europe, he kept tabs of people donning baseball caps, T-shirts, or other baseball-related apparel. Using this admittedly limited research method, he came to a few non-scientific, yet surprisingly accurate, conclusions that have been corroborated by many other Americans abroad, regardless of where they have traveled:

1. If the article of baseball apparel in question was from any of the other MLB teams, the wearer was certainly American, or a non-American who had lived in that particular city, or had some other close connection with that city. (Case in point: the Cleveland Indians' Chief Wahoo cap has never quite caught on as worldwide chic.)

2. If the article in question was a Yankee item, seven times out of ten, the wearer was NOT an American.

3. The non-Americans who donned Yankee apparel were generally obnoxious, behaved rather badly, and very often publicly badmouthed the U.S. as an imperialistic superpower.

4. Most of the Americans who donned ball caps from other teams acted like obnoxious Americans as well. Let's face facts: To most of the civilized world, America as a country—though undoubtedly the most powerful on Earth—is akin to an overgrown and spoiled teenager. And we act like it. Not to say this is a negative evaluation. Quite the contrary. We're proud to be the pranksters of the world. We're the carefree vagabonds with a short history and even shorter attention spans. And we're okay with that stereotype. It suits us well, and we're comfortable with our roles as funny men (and women) to the world.

We have since drawn a few unpopular, but no less true deductions from this data. First of all, the Yankees merchandizing market is worldwide—with partnerships stretching from Europe to Japan. No other team can claim this or benefit from it. Secondly, to many peoples of the world, the *NY* on the Yankee ball cap and pinstriped jersey and, perhaps most of all, the very name "Yankees" have become synonymous with the most unflattering side of American values, culture, and unfettered capitalism and imperialistic intent abroad. It's akin to the exportation of McDonalds and Coke, U.S. Military superiority, and third-rate Hollywood movie trash starring the likes of Jean Claude Van Damme available at a Wal-Mart near you all rolled into one nicely packaged and heavily advertised scary pop culture sandwich. And the symbol of it all is the nice little NY interlock that the Yankees and their spawn don across the globe.

> **If there ever was in the history of humanity an enemy who was truly universal, an enemy whose acts and moves trouble the entire world, threaten the entire world, attack the entire world in any way or another, that real and really universal enemy is precisely Yankee imperialism.**

> **—Fidel Castro**

The wave of backlash against it all is growing to be just as powerful. An archeologist recently traveled to the Islands of Indonesia where tribes undiscovered by Western man live as they have for thousands of years. He lived with one tribe and studied them and was surprised to find a ritual that occurred in the first week of April every year where the tribe would gather around a fire made ceremoniously of Yankee caps that had fallen from merchant ships by the boxful and washed upon their shores. The tribe would encircle the conflagration and chant (in their native tongue of course) "Not again! Not again! Not again! Babe Ruth sucks."

KEVIN: Sounds like a few parties you went to in college, eh?

JOSH: Sounds like every party I went to in college.

But seriously, there can be no doubt that the Yankees of New York have benefited from the near perfect symmetry of their name and its tie to America's early history. Remember: "Yankee Doodle" was a pejorative term that the British put on the colonial Americans with whom they were at war. These improvisational-minded revolutionaries spun it on its head adopted the moniker, "I'm a Yankee Doodle Dandy," and wore it as a badge of honor. What could be more American than taking a knock and spinning it into a positive image?

> **The Yankee is one who, if he once gets his teeth set on a thing, all creation can't make him let go.**
>
> **—Ralph Waldo Emerson**

But these revolutionary Yankees came from *all* thirteen of the colonies. We were all Yanks back then, and to some degree, we're all Yanks now . . . at least in the eyes of the world. And the irony is not lost on us that the area of the country that still most closely identifies with the term Yankee is New England. Not only do Bostonians proudly consider themselves Yankees, but the term is still defined as particular to the New Englander in most dictionaries.

KEVIN: Hear that Red Sox Nation? You're all Yankees.

JOSH: You think you're the first to come up with that tired old joke?

Of course, the term Yankee has evolved over the years. Leading up to the American Civil War, the term "Yankee" came to symbolize to the American South all that was wrong with the Northern states, and once again became a slur. Damn Yankees. Southerners were so upset with the way they were being economically manipulated by the Yankees of the North that they seceded from the Union.

Now, while we're not going to get into a lengthy discussion of the rights and wrongs of secession, it is interesting to note that as baseball fans, we share many of those same sentiments now. Slavery was wrong and was the worst thing that humankind has ever created for itself, but the more subtle forms of economic, political, and imperial subjugation of the little guy by the big guy cannot be tolerated either. And the Yankees of New York are certainly guilty of this, at least as far as baseball is concerned. The question becomes: Do we as Americans want this Yankee symbol to continue to represent us? Does it accurately portray who we are as Americans?

As we have pointed out previously, the New York Yankees baseball club is perhaps the most perfectly named team in the history of the sporting world. Who can deny that had the Yankees kept their original nickname, the "Highlanders," they would never have achieved the worldwide fame that they now enjoy? Well, they may have been a big hit in Scotland, but that's not a big country for baseball. The links, yes. Baseball, not so much.

And after all, New York is the largest city in America, and to the many immigrants who have fled to New York for hundreds of years and to those they left behind, New York is the very symbol of freedom, capitalism, and the American Dream. It has been the gateway for many to enter the New World and the beacon that symbolizes the American dream across the globe.

As America's renown has spread worldwide, the aptly named Yankees' fame has spread right alongside it. America, New York, and baseball: To many around the globe, that's the sum of their knowledge of this great land of ours. Babe Ruth's big appetites for home runs, food, drink, women, and even life itself helped deliver the message that America was an up-and-coming power. We were young, strong, uninhibited, and had that can-do attitude that war-ravaged Europe sorely lacked. There was nothing we felt we were incapable of, and, as a result, there was little that held us back. The Yankees were like starved teenagers that were eating their parents out of house and home. But who can blame a teen for his appetites? "He's just a growing boy," folks would say. And so, Americans felt good about their hero, Ruth, and his symbolic significance and bought into it wholesale.

But things changed somewhere along the line. The Yankees' big appetite was transformed from growing teen into that of a gluttonous and spoiled despot. It's difficult to say exactly when and where this transmutation occurred. Winning championships at any cost, even at the heavy cost of buying them outright, has become accepted behavior, almost par for the course, even demanded by Yankee fans. Do they now care *how* they win? No, they care only *that* they win. Nothing else seems to matter. Yankee fans have devolved from gracious and appreciative winners to spoiled, expectant, and ill-behaved brats.

What would Yankees like Gehrig and DiMaggio say about these latter day Yankee teams? They would be disgraced, as all Yankee fans should be. Why? Because the Yankees have at long last killed off the American Dream that their name has come to symbolize so well. Sure, Steinbrenner isn't breaking any rules by putting an All-Star at every position (and a few on the bench) as well as a potential Cy Young Award winner at all five spots in the starting rotation—and don't forget the All-Star closer.

But the American Dream is the dream of us all. It's the dream that tells us that even the lowest of us can succeed if we work hard enough to be the best. At the end of the American Dream is a land where the Pittsburgh Pirates can win the World Series if they are indeed the team that wants to succeed the most. But the Yankees are leading the way to make sure that this can never happen. Only the top-flight teams that can compete with the Yanks—the Red Sox, the Mets, the Dodgers, the Angels, and a handful of others—are wealthy enough to be competitive each and every year. For teams in the bottom third tier of payroll, well, they might as well be playing in the Independent Northern League for all the chance they have.

It's this elitism that bothers us most about the money that the Yankees spend. By transforming baseball into more of a money game than ever, the Yankees are leading the charge toward making baseball irrelevant. It's becoming like the English Soccer League, where the Premiership is filled with the wealthiest teams, and the second tier is for the second-class teams that can never (even with the relegation rule) become competitive. It's downright un-American, bad for baseball, and even anti-Yankee, if we may be so bold as to suggest.

Every time I see a Yankee's hat, I see a swastika just a little off kilter.

—Red Sox pitcher Bill Lee

And this heartily un-American death that has come to the American Dream in baseball affects the fans as well. We all complain when ticket prices and hot dog prices go up, yet rarely do we sound a peep when our team signs a highly priced free agent. No, that we consider a victory. Meanwhile, the game is getting so expensive that you have to have a corporate connection to get a decent seat. Corporate names now hang from our glorious ballparks that were once named for the game's great teams, owners, and the neighborhoods where the ballparks were located. Well, maybe some of the owners weren't so great, but at least they were affiliated with baseball and not phone networks, banks, and other corporate power brokers.

Bringing huge dollars into the game has cheapened it and distanced the average fan—the fan who used to be the lifeblood of the game. We're not going to go on and on about the "good old days" that we were not alive to experience. There are plenty of other books that blather on romantically about the lost glory days of baseball. But consider this: Tickets were available to all in those days, and team loyalty was as high on the part of players as it has always been on the part of fans. We can all admit that the loss of these two aspects of the game have made the game less than what it once was.

But the worst of it all is that, although many people consider the times we live in now to be the second golden age of baseball, only the folks with the most gold get to enjoy it. Whether you love the Yankees or hate them, you must admit that spending $280 dollars for a family of four to attend a game, park, and eat modestly at the ballpark is a bit cuckoo. And worse, this change in the game that has been led by the Yankees has been promulgated at the expense of the common fans, the everyday Joes and Janes, the soul of the sport, the nation and the very fabric of American culture.

It's sad, really. Does America no longer represent the truth that there can be a home for everyone here? Does it not symbolize that people of all ethnic, religious, and economical backgrounds are equal? We each get a vote, and each vote counts equally: rich or poor, Jew or Gentile, straight, gay, bi or transgendered. Is America and true democracy not the model that the world must follow in order for us all to live in peace and harmony? Why, yes it is. Yes, on all accounts. So shouldn't we all have equal access to the ballpark?

JOSH: You can say what you want about us, but I'm not going to stand here and let anyone badmouth the United States of America. Gentlemen!
KEVIN: Isn't that from a scene in *Animal House*?

But as the saying goes, "absolute power corrupts, absolutely." And the Yankees have continued their pattern of abusing their power within the baseball world.

For an example of this unholy domination, consider the CBS television show *The Clubhouse*, which premiered in fall of 2004. The show was about a batboy for the New York Empires, a baseball team set in New York City. Producers for the show were told in the middle of production during its first season that they would either have to change their choice of pinstriped uniforms or risk a copyright infringement lawsuit brought on by the Yankees. Apparently the current Yankee ownership has little love for CBS, the former owners of the team.

Now, don't get us wrong, but aren't there two teams in New York that wear pinstripes at home? And aren't there about a dozen other teams that wear them regularly as well? You see, the Yankees are a powerful enough entity that all they have to do is flex their monetary muscle and anyone smaller that gets in their way gets crushed. That's not democracy, that's fascism.

In this pinstripes debacle, the Yankees have proven that they realize how important symbols are. And somewhere along the line, the Yankee management must have concluded that the Yankees invented the pinstriped uniform. Well, we've provided (with a hand from our friends at the National Baseball Hall of Fame in Cooperstown) a little history lesson for those Yankees out there who think their boys are the sole owners and inventors of pinstripes.

National League teams from Detroit and Washington first donned pinstripes in 1888, as did the Brooklyn team of the American Association during the same season. Newsflash: There were no New York Yankees in 1888! This was a full fifteen years before the team that would eventually become the Yankees was even incorporated into a ball club. The first team in the twentieth century to wear the pinstripes was the Boston Doves, the team that later became known as the Braves, in the year 1907. The first Yankee/Highlander team to wear pinstripes took the field five years later, in 1912. After skipping the 1913 and 1914 seasons, the Yanks once again took up the pinstripes in 1915 and have worn them ever since.

Certainly, the Yankees have consistently worn pinstripes for a long while now. But did the Yankees invent them? No. Were they the first to wear them? No. Do they have a trademark on them? Well, teams had been wearing them for twenty-four seasons before the Yankees jumped on the bandwagon. And other teams wear them still. So, do the Yankees have the right to tell people what they can or cannot wear on a television show, even if it is set in New York? Again, a resounding No!

But it is exactly this type of Yankee bullying that comes to symbolize all that is wrong with baseball in America. Is it not enough to have won more World Series championships than the next two closest teams combined? Apparently not for the gluttonous Yanks. And remember, gluttony is perhaps the deadliest of the seven deadly sins. Just ask Elvis.

To be manager of the Yankees under the malevolent dictatorship of George Steinbrenner is like being married to Zsa Zsa Gabor—the union is short and sweet.

—Bob Rubin, sportswriter

The Yankees are like a big fat Gordon Gecko (Michael Douglas's character in the film *Wall Street*) when he says: "Greed is good. Greed will help fix the broken corporation of America." And we all know what happened to Gordon Gecko . . . and Michael Milken. Unfettered greed is neither good for America nor good for America's game. Ambition—that's good. Competitiveness is good. Fair play—also good. Greed, rarely, if ever, is good.

Another irony is that most of the Yankee fans we know cannot see this reality for the life of them. We have Yankee friends (we know, we're embarrassed by them as well) whose mantra is, "Peace, Love, and Yankee Baseball." We suspect that these deluded individuals don't even actually believe the false words they extol. They say them because the Yankees are so well known to be in opposition to peaceful and brotherly good will that the comment comes off as funny. And it does. In the meantime, these Yankee fans blindly stick their heads in the sand when we point out to them all the ills of Yankee excess and greed. How does the biblical saying go? There are none so blind as those who shall not see.

> **Baseball is like the United States of America. It's too big to be loused up by one man and one monumental mistake.**
>
> **—Former White Sox owner Arthur C. Allyn**

But no single person can come to an excess of power without the assistance of others. Perhaps, the only thing more pathetic than Steinbrenner's lust for power and influence over the baseball world is that of his cronies and cohorts, namely: the other (twenty or so, not all of them) owners (and the commissioner) who secretly want to be Georgie Porgie. These misguided men and women earn tremendous salaries from their baseball teams, even the ones from the small markets—don't let them fool you. Otherwise, they'd sell. After all, it's a business. As one player (who claimed an IQ of 160) pointed out:

> **I have a hard time believing athletes are overpriced. If an owner is losing money, give it up. It's a business. I have trouble figuring out why owners would stay in if they're losing money.**
>
> **—Reggie Jackson**

Well, we can agree with the second half of this quote at least. Players are overpriced, there's no doubt about it. But Jackson's thinking on this matter highlights not only the problem with the game as it stands today but also the fact that these owners are making money—indeed smaller sums when compared to Steinbrenner, but the owners get paid first, before they have a chance to whine to the press about not having anything left over to compete for championships.

So captivated are these wannabe owners by the Yankees' success that they have deluded themselves into thinking that they will be able to grow their own mystique into some equally vast empire. Or perhaps they're content to sit around the table of King George, fighting over the meaty table scraps of Yankee excess.

But in order to get to the table, they must serve at the pleasure of the top dog, and that stinking, flea-bitten, mangy mutt, is Steinbrenner. These pitiful owners who kowtow to Steinbrenner's every desire can only be described as bush league. Why can't they realize that they are minor warlords in these skirmishes, dancing on the strings pulled by Genghis George? And worse, that, if united, they could change baseball for the better—for fans, players, owners, and for the future good of the game.

[Orlando Hernandez is] a very lucky man. He escapes the dictatorial reign of a ruthless tyrant and ends up working for George Steinbrenner.

—David Letterman

Sure they talk tough about George behind his back. We've all heard them make many of the same claims that we make here in this book. But when push comes to shove, George has been incredibly effective at dividing and conquering, at pitting his flunkies against one another in order to get what he wants in the end. For whether they intend to or not, the owners, though they own voting majority, end up doing Georgie's bidding. And together they are killing the American Dream for us all.

The founding fathers of this country developed a highly complicated system of checks and balances in order to protect all Americans from tyranny. The President must answer to the Supreme Court and Congress. Wall Street must answer to the SEC. The drug industry must answer to the FDA. But to whom do the Yankees answer? Who monitors Steinbrenner's activities? A bunch of "yes" men and women and a commissioner whose interests lie clearly with the owners. The word "lapdogs" certainly applies but barely does the situation justice.

> **I'm not very smart. I think I can prove that. Who would accept a job with Marge Schott's dog, Ted Turner, and George Steinbrenner as your boss?**
>
> **—Peter Ueberroth, former commissioner**

But without a better system of checks and balances, things stay just the way they are, and just the way Georgie likes them. Let's face the reality that baseball has been corrupt for quite some time now (steroids, gambling, drug scandals of the '80s, unfettered greed, unfair play), and it's not going to get any better until the other owners put pressure on Bud Selig to do his job and stand up to the owner that benefits the most from the status quo, King George, exalted ruler of the Evil Empire.

Boxing was once the most followed sport in America. So, too, was horse racing. But years of corruption that went unchecked and unchanged ruined both of these sports and left them with all the significance of the next winner on *American Idol*. Does anyone really care about these sports anymore? Not like they used to. The same thing will happen to baseball if the current version of the game, spearheaded by Steinbrenner and his cronies, is allowed to continue.

Chapter Sixteen

The Greedy Glutton's Curse

It's Kevin here again, with another story.

Some people thought I'd be upset when the Yankees traded for Alex Rodriguez (or perhaps better stated, Steinbrenner stole Pay-Rod from both Texas Ranger owner Tom Hicks—who actually pays the Yankees a considerable sum for Rodriguez to play for them—and from the Red Sox, who had their trade nixed by the Players Association and League officials). After all, Pay-Rod is the most expensive and arguably the best player in baseball whose name isn't Barry Bonds, and he is a former Mariner. People that know me were afraid to even call in the weeks after the trade, certain that I would be in the foulest of my Yankee-hating moods. They were wrong.

I was elated when the Yankees acquired A-Rod, not because I agreed that Rodriguez is a big-time player who belongs in a big-time market (as the pro-Yankee media spun the deal). And certainly not because I thought Rodriguez would help the Yanks win, which he undoubtedly will.

Not a chance. I called friends back in Seattle and said to them, "Isn't this the greatest?" They agreed, one and all, that the Pay-Rod trade was by far the best thing for the Yankees, and the best thing for all of baseball.

Normally, of course, we *would have been livid* at the Yankees for acquiring yet another of the game's best players. But not this time. Our unlikely reaction to yet another Yankee player grab came about because of an event that had taken place years before. A dark secret that only the writing of this book has prompted me to extol.

I was living is Seattle, you see, and the Mariners had built a team with as much raw talent as any in recent memory. Ken Griffey, Jr., Edgar Martinez, Randy Johnson, Jay Buhner, Jeff Nelson, and Tino Martinez were the core members, and all of them had been brought up through the Mariners' system or had been acquired very early in their careers. This was to be our dynasty . . . our team . . . our reward for nearly twenty seasons of suffering with the Mariners, or as they were commonly known back then, the best AAA club in the big leagues.

And best of all, perhaps, they were led by a real manager, the fiery and entertaining Lou Piniella. "Sweet Lou," the former Yankee player and manager, was going to lead the Mariners to the World Series. And it was going to be good.

You must remember, not only had the M's been the laughingstocks of the league for the whole of their history, but there were also hardly any players on those early teams worth remembering. It was a franchise that had no "franchise player" whose name was synonymous with the city. When you think of Williams, you immediately think Boston. Gwynn, San Diego. Ripken, Baltimore. DiMaggio, New York. These are men who have become so symbolic of the city in which they played we don't even need to use their first names and you know who they are and what city they represent.

The Seattle Mariners had no such superstar. Sure, they had some good players, some of whom they even held onto like Alvin Davis and Harold Reynolds. But still . . . there was no Mantle, Ruth, or DiMaggio for Seattle to celebrate.

As I have detailed previously, the Mariners were to lose three potential Hall of Famers in three straight seasons, any of whom could have been that franchise player. Randy Johnson felt he could better win in the postseason elsewhere, never really liking the Mariners organization. And Griffey claimed that he wanted to play in Cincinnati, the city of his youth, and for the Reds, the team for which his dad was the hitting coach. And even though everyone in Seattle knew the reason for his demand to be traded was that his hitting at Seattle's new Safeco Field had taken a nose dive, can you really blame a guy who just wants to go home?

It was during the 2000 season that Alex Rodriguez made it known that he would be open to offers made possible by free agency at season's end, if he wasn't traded first. He still claimed to love Seattle and the Mariners, and all they had done for him. Even so, most folks in the Northwest felt the gloomy specter above our heads yet again—that we were about to lose yet another guy who could have led us to the World Series and in the process symbolized our city to the world of sports.

Seattle could have traded away A-Rod during the 2000 season and received plenty in return for him, as they had done with Griffey and Johnson, but instead they chose to trust in Rodriguez's words of praise for the city and kept him through the playoffs, in hopes that they would make it to the World Series with their star and be able to re-sign him at the end of the season. A-Rod delivered, hitting .409 with two dingers in the losing ALCS effort against the Yankees. After the season was over, Seattle offered their ascending star more money than any player in baseball: $18.4 million per season for five years. It was the best the M's could possibly offer, but not nearly enough to feed A-Rod's ego. After all, A-Rod's agent was Scott Boras, notorious for driving player salaries through the roof. But with regard to A-Rod, Boras turned out to be right.

The truth was that A-Rod never wanted to be a Mariner in the first place. He'd asked the team not to draft him while he was still in high school in Miami. There was no loyalty to the city or the team for all both had done for Alex. No, sadly the thing that motivated A-Rod the most, it turned out, was money. He remained healthy, didn't get traded, and avoided the Mariners' offer, then he cashed in—big time. A-Rod signed a ten-year deal with the Texas Rangers (a division rival!), worth more than a quarter of a billion dollars. It was disgustingly sick money. So much so that hundreds of articles detailed the ridiculous sum that Pay-Rod (as he was starting to be known) would make: tens of thousands for every at bat, thousands for every ball pitched to him, and even great big gobs of money left over just for lacing up his shoes. And to make matters worse, Boras had even negotiated an "escalation" clause into Pay-Rod's new contract that stated that if another player were to sign a contract for more money, then Pay-Rod's salary must always be at least one dollar higher.

After all, if it's all about money, then the best player should get the biggest slice of the pie, right?

This was too much for my friends in Seattle and me to take. Even though I'd left town a few years before, we had made arrangements to get together on my trip home and do something about this preposterous nightmare.

Sure, the folks at Safeco who dumped monopoly money off the third deck like confetti when A-Rod returned as a Ranger got some laughs and some good airplay on *SportsCenter*. One guy attached a large bill to a fishing pole in an attempt to lure Rodriguez toward the only bait he seemed to understand, also garnering a snide chuckle. But we wanted more. We needed to do something big, make a statement that would be equal to the injury that he caused us, our team, and our beloved city. In a word, we wanted revenge—a quarter of a billion dollars' worth of revenge.

So, the meeting commenced in a friend's living room, with beer and ESPN on in the background, still reporting the excesses of Pay-Rod's salary.

But what could we, lowly fans, do to show players like Pay-Rod that they were killing the game we loved? We tossed around hundreds of ideas, ranging from framing Pay-Rod in a prostitution scandal a la Marv Albert to a letter writing campaign to smear his good name. All options were dishonest, highly illegal, or far too ineffectual. After three hours wasted, we began to lose hope. It seemed that we could do nothing. We would have to accept our fate. Pay-Rod was going to be a great player, make great money, and have a life overfilled with bounty, while Seattle suffered.

Then one of my friends, *Damian* (not his real name), proffered the most bizarre suggestion of them all: "Why don't we cast a voodoo curse on the greedy glutton to keep him from ever winning the World Series? No one as greedy as Pay-Rod deserves to win a World Series, nor does any team greedy enough to sign him."

After the initial laughter died down, shouts echoed throughout the living room: "You can't be serious," "Snap out of it," and "Have another beer, Damian."

"I'm dead serious," he said. "I know a guy who can do this. A-Rod will be the albatross strapped to the neck of any team that signs him."

Well, the sane members of our posse nearly laughed Damian and his foolish idea out of the room. It was ludicrous, wrong, and certainly not worthy of our serious consideration. Damian pleaded that it was the only effective thing we could do, but we wouldn't budge.

"Fine," he said. "If none of you has the guts to help, I'll do it myself." He left abruptly, and drove off in his truck.

A month or so later, after Damian returned from a vacation in New Orleans, we all got an e-mail saying that all had been taken care of, and that a real live curse had been cast on Rodriguez and any team stupid enough to sign him. Damian said it was called the "Curse of the Greedy Glutton Pay-Rod," but would not go into the details of whether he'd consulted a voodoo witch doctor, an Indian Shaman, or knew a high priestess of Santeria. He simply told us to watch and enjoy the fruits of his efforts.

"You'll all thank me one day," he wrote. Of course, we thought Damian had finally gone completely coconuts. But looking at the evidence since then, we're not so certain any more:

2001: The Mariners play their first season without Pay-Rod, and win 116 games, tying MLB's all-time record. A-Rod heads for Texas and three seasons of languishing in last place with the Rangers.

2004: A-Rod is nearly traded from Texas to the Red Sox, but the Sox avert the disaster of another curse laid on their heads, as Pay-Rod becomes a Yankee in an underhanded debacle. Texas goes on to their best season in recent memory, narrowly missing the playoffs and putting together one of the youngest and most promising infields in baseball. The Red Sox pull off the greatest comeback in playoff history, defeating the Yankees in the ALCS after being down 3–0. Never before had the Sox defeated the Yankees in *any* significant playoff series. The Red Sox go on to win their first World Series in eighty-six years, smashing the most feared and gripping curse in all of baseball and in all of sport: The Curse of the Bambino. And the Yankees, who had won the first three games of the ALCS with relative ease, whose payroll was so excessive and inflated, whose offensive firepower was unmatched in either league, suddenly couldn't get a hit to save their sorry butts. In four straight games they were the chokers, the losers, the Red Sox and Cubbies and every other cursed club in baseball all rolled into one.

Sure, we doubted our crazy friend, Damian, too. But not any longer. The very cosmos have obviously shifted dramatically. Most people think it occurred sometime during the 2004 ALCS. But a cosmic shift of this magnitude was years in the making. Just ask the Texas Rangers, the Mariners, the Red Sox, and even the 2004 Yankees. Something has changed in the universe, and it has stunned New Yorkers to their very core. They were left dumbfounded and with that question on their lips that has plagued so many other teams, "Why did this happen to us?"

Well, New York, you've got your answer. It seems perfect kismet to us that the greedy glutton A-Rod should align forces with the equally greedy glutton Steinbrenner. With the curse firmly in place, it was like killing two birds with one stone. Now the stain of this powerful curse would be right where it belonged: on the heads of the most avarice-ridden franchise in all of baseball.

The only stage I need is the World Series.

—Alex Rodriguez

So beware Yankees and Yankee fans everywhere. The Curse of the Greedy Glutton Pay-Rod is now on your doorstep. Don't say we didn't warn you. And don't discount the power of this curse. A-Rod may break every record in the books, but you'll never win a World Series as long as Pay-Rod is on your team. And with luck, George will sour on Pay-Rod like he did Winfield and try something shady to get himself booted out of baseball.

But, if the Yankees do manage to win a World Series with Pay-Rod on the team, Yankee fans must then live with the knowledge that their team is in league with a much darker power than that of my friend Damian. Discomforting thought, isn't it?

Chapter Seventeen

An Open Letter to Yankee Fans

Dear fans of the New York Yankees baseball club:

Please allow us to apologize for having fun at your expense throughout the entirety of this book. Although it was fun, to be sure, we mean you no disrespect. If you're asking yourself the "Why does everyone hate us so much?" question (that we definitely hope you are asking), here's a little story that might help you understand why America hates you and everything you do with the burning fire of a thousand suns.

On a baseball road trip to Jacobs Field to see the Tribe take on the Yankees, our friends, Alan Mosovsky and Bruce Stollings, sat down to enjoy an evening of baseball, Cleveland-style. This was during the 2002 season, the one that followed the attacks of 9-11-01, and Alan and Bruce—though sworn Yankee-haters—had found it a tad difficult during this time to root against the New York club. In fact, the goodwill of the entire country was still on the side of the Yankees, having carried over from 2001. New Yorkers had all our sympathies and our prayers with them for all they had been through. And if the Bronx Bombers could make New Yorkers happy by winning another World Series, well then, Yankee-haters across the land seemed willing to keep their traps temporarily shut for the good of the USA and for your fair city.

But keep in mind that this was an entire season later, and after a full game of withholding their traditional Yankee boos and jeers, Alan and Bruce spotted an eighty-year-old woman with a T-shirt that said "I ♥ NY" printed across the front. She was walking the aisles of the stadium, and the Cleveland crowd stood and cheered for her as she passed. The woman raised her hand in acknowledgment of the crowd like a beloved politician, smiling and waiving to her fans, who applauded her message of goodwill.

Our friends grew miffed. After all, it had been more than a full season since 9-11, the Yankees had not won the World Series in 2001, and Bruce and Dave wondered how long this Yankee love-fest had to be endured. They'd withheld their Yankee-hating barbs and traditional shouting of "Der-ek Je-ter—O-ver-ra-ted!" Clap clap, clap-clap-clap. But now this? A kindly old woman doling out Yankee goodwill like a parade clown dishes out candy? When would the insanity of Yankee support end? Alan and Bruce were ashamed for this woman, for the Cleveland fans, and for the entire baseball world.

But as the old woman drew closer, they noticed that folks only cheered for her once she had walked past them. As she passed our friends, they notice that printed across the back of her shirt was printed, "But I STILL Hate Them Yankees!" Alan and Bruce eagerly joined the crowd by standing and cheering her on as she passed by. Their faith in Cleveland fans, in baseball fans, in fact, their very faith in humanity was restored that day.

This example, perhaps above all else, should demonstrate to you what is wrong with your baseball team. After 9-11 everyone was with you, on your side—even your harshest of critics. And now, once again, everyone is against you. Yankees fans, you must wonder to yourselves, in the darkness of your lonely rooms: How did we squander all that precious Yankee goodwill?

To us, this story illustrates a few points. First, New York is a great city, maybe the greatest city. But you can love New York and still hate the Yankees. In fact, you should do exactly that. America still supports New York 100 percent in all efforts against all non-baseball-related enemies, but we do not support your tyrannical Yankees. Second, in the days following 9-11, the Yankees truly had the country behind them in the same way that the media would have us believe is the case every year. For those few weeks of September when baseball helped to assuage the pains of a nation, New York led the way, and we all rallied behind them. We were united, and our differences seemed minor compared to the fact that we were all Americans. And baseball made us feel like Americans once again—even Yankee baseball.

But something changed over the course of that year. Rather than returning the nation's gesture of goodwill and support, the Yankees moved even more toward trying to buy a championship. In fact, the Yankees payroll has more than doubled since the 2000 season, the last time they won a World Series. Instead of returning the olive branch that the country had offered (like the city of New York did), the Yankees decided that they would simply go out and buy another World Series, or perhaps attain one by hostile corporate takeover. Certainly, the rest of the baseball world recognized the Yankees' "Me First—Gimme Gimme" attitude demonstrated by the alarming rate that the Yankees pursued the game's top free agents. Again, while spending ridiculous money on free agents is still technically within the rules of the game, the way the Yankees have been going about it makes a mockery of those rules. Take the following examples.

After not winning the World Series in 2001, Steinbrenner was able to outbid the Oakland A's for free agent AL MVP Jason Giambi by offering a seven-year, $120 million contract *and* a no-trade clause. Big Stein also added David Wells, Raul Mondesi, and Robin Ventura, just for good measure.

When the Yanks didn't win the Series again in 2002, George, perhaps still angered by losing out to Seattle on the bid to sign the Japanese phenom Ichiro in 2001, went right out and got the two most highly sought after and expensive free agents on the global market: Hideki Matsui, known as "Godzilla" in his native Japan, and the then latest defector from Cuba, Jose Contreras.

Again the Yankees didn't win the World Series in 2003, so King George went out and acquired the most expensive player in all of team sports, the man who was making such ridiculous money that his Texas Ranger team had no prayer of success with him on the roster: Pay-Rod, er, we mean A-Rod, Alex Rodriguez. The trade was so lopsided that it has Texas covering a significant portion of Pay-Rod's salary (supposedly for being the best player in the game) while he plays for the league's most successful and storied franchise. See anything wrong with this picture? Throw in Kevin Brown, Javier Vazquez, Gary Sheffield, Tom Gordon, Paul Quantrill, and Kenny Lofton as icing on the 2004 cake. Since Sheffield had MVP numbers, that's some pretty sweet icing.

And when the Yanks didn't win the World Series yet again in 2004, Big Stein acquired the Big Unit, Randy Johnson, the most dominant left-hander of his era. Again, throw in Carl Pavano and Jaret Wright, just for insurance purposes. And why not take Tino Martinez back, too, just in case the Yanks might be able to weasel out of their contract with Giambi after he admitted to using performance-enhancing drugs.

All of these players were considered the top free agents and trade-available players in their respective years. In retrospect, some of these players have been mistakes for the Yankees, while others have been huge successes. But to say that George is flushing money down the toilet doesn't even begin to address what he's been doing. King George is piling up Yankee money with a bulldozer, dropping gasoline on the mound with a crop duster, and burning up the Yankee Elysian Fields in an inferno of grotesque waste and gluttony. How many years will it be until the Yankees' roster consists of all twenty-five of the top player salaries?

> **KEVIN:** I thought we were already there.
> **JOSH:** Don't put anything past King George.

There are teams who would be pleased to have the bucks to acquire one of these players in a five-year period—like the Orioles, for example. If Baltimore made just one of the mistakes that the Yankees made, like the Giambi, Brown, or Contreras mistakes, they would have had to pay for that mistake for seasons to come. This calamity actually happened to the Orioles when they signed Albert Belle. In 1998 Belle was a top free agent playing for the White Sox, a big hitter that demanded top money from the market. Belle signed a five-year deal with the Orioles for $65 million. After a mediocre 1999 campaign, Belle was diagnosed in 2000 with a degenerative hip condition. He never recovered from his injuries and left baseball early. Even though the Orioles had insurance to pay the injured Belle part of his salary, their purse strings were drawn tight until they could get out from under the weight of it—through the end of the 2003 season. Then what did the Orioles do the minute they were free of the Belle fiasco? They went out and broke the bank again to acquire Miguel Tejada and Javy Lopez. Some teams never learn. But only the Yankees have the money to endure mistakes this big without suffering any noticeable drop off in play. And they dump big salaried players who have been colossal failures nearly every season, without breaking a sweat. It's all part of their economic plan.

What George never understood was that the goodwill gesture that America offered his team *did mean something*. Even the most ardent Yankee-hater is still a fan of the game of baseball.

So Yankee fans, you ask yourself, "Why do you all hate us?" After all, the Yankees are just like any other team, only more successful, right? Wrong. Please allow us to ask of you a few tough questions, in order to more fully answer this conundrum.

> **QUESTION #1:** Do you ever complain about the skyrocketing costs of tickets, hot dogs, and Crunch and Munch—err, we mean Cracker Jack—at Yankee Stadium?
> **ANSWER #1:** Sure, we do at our own parks as well. The game is getting so expensive that you have to be Donald Trump to get a decent ticket.
>
> **QUESTION #2:** Do you hearken back to the days when the Yankees were Yankees, good guys, brought up through the system and into the game as Yankee rookies, or do you care only about winning, regardless of how you win?
> **ANSWER #2:** Baseball would be much improved if teams stocked their rosters primarily with home-grown players rather than "rent-a-veterans" bought from other ball clubs.
>
> **QUESTION #3:** Which current big-league owner would you least like to leave your children with for the evening?
> **ANSWER #3:** George Steinbrenner. It's not even close. Two hours with the Big Stein and your kid will be leveraging his schoolmates for their milk money.

QUESTION #4: What are you prepared to do about it?
ANSWER #4: Follow *Kevin and Josh's Eight-Point Plan for Yankee Fans to Help Save Baseball.*

It's like our good friend, Tom White, once said: "Rooting for the Yankees is like going to a casino and betting on the house." It's simply bad form to everyone else at the craps table to bet the "No Pass" line. And face it: the Yankees have more money, power, and influence than any Vegas casino.

And aside from the obvious futility of betting against the house that Tom's point illustrates—the deck being overwhelmingly stacked in its favor—it also speaks to the fact that the Yankees (like the house) run the show, and we all know it. We all know the house is going to win in the end, so why would anyone root for the inevitable? Isn't the point of gambling to take the house for all you can?

All kidding aside, let's face facts for a moment. With all due respect to small towns across this great land, the American city that most exemplifies the American Dream is New York City. After all, on New Year's Eve, we're watching the ball drop from Times Square, not Main Street in Dubuque, Iowa, right? And the American Dream, briefly stated, is the idea that we can offer a better life for our children than we ourselves had, or our parents had, and that with hard work and a firm resolve to follow the rules of this great land of ours, we will succeed in America.

And who could be in a better position to demand change in the structure of America's great national pastime than the fans of its most successful franchise: New York Yankees fans. If the fate of baseball has always been in the hands of the Yankees, then who better to lead baseball back to the fertile grounds of its better days? So without further adieu, Yankees fans, we proudly present for your approval:

183

KEVIN AND JOSH'S EIGHT-POINT PLAN FOR YANKEE FANS TO HELP SAVE BASEBALL:

Point #1: Welcome a Third New York Team to Baseball.

Redividing the Big Apple pie won't solve all of the problems with the Yankees dominating the cash flow in baseball, but it's a step in the right direction. While Big Stein will likely veto any team that enters "his" market and cuts into "his" pie piece (we're reminded of that cartoon where a slice of pie is offered and the rest of the pie is taken, leaving only the single slice for everyone else), who died and gave King George veto power anyway? As Rodney Dangerfield (Al Czervik) says in the movie *Caddy Shack*, "Who elected him Pope of this dump?" And while we realize that getting another baseball team into any of the five boroughs, New Jersey, or even southern Connecticut is going to be a tough sell, if it doesn't happen, Yanks fans who are sick of the status quo can always convert to the Mets.

> **KEVIN:** Meet the Mets. Meet the Mets. Step right up and greet the Mets.
> **JOSH:** I don't like the Mets much either.

Point #2: Admit That the Yankees Are the Evil Empire.

Although it may be a tough pill to swallow, look at the facts and admit the truth. Perhaps this will help: Remember the storm troopers in *Star Wars*' Evil Empire were clones that mindlessly followed orders. Only when the dark veil of the Emperor's spell was finally lifted did they suddenly have free will and freedom of thought. They were suddenly able to make their own moral decisions and shape their own behaviors. Doesn't this sound liberating? And once you do this, Big Stein loses all his powers. Who wouldn't find a rehabilitated

184

Steinbrenner cute and lovable, just as when Lord Vader removed his dark helmet and showed the world his smiling and pulpy misshapen skull at the end of *Return of the Jedi*.

Point #3: Get Over the Idea That Yankee-Haters Are Simply Jealous.

Yankee-haters of the world have a canon of legitimate complaints against your ball club. We're not jealous of you—okay, we are, but there's so much more to it that just that. It is the false pride that Yankee fans have, their crass behavior, and the team's attempts to buy championships that we despise. Your owner plays by a set of rules that keep a corrupt and broken system flailing along. When you come to see things our way, you'll realize that we have your best interests at heart, as well as those of all fans of the game. Creating a more even playing field for all teams will go a long way to repairing the damage that your team has done to the sport. And don't fear, your Yankees will still be heavily favored, just not quite as dominant.

Point #4: Help Bring Back Real Yankee Pride.

Renounce the shallow victories that buying championships has brought your once great Yankee team. Write letters to sports editors, complain in the streets, lustily "boo" players who disgrace the Yankee uniform and ideals. Wouldn't a championship with players who weren't arrogant, overpaid mercenaries be a tad more appealing than what's been going on lately in Yankeeland? Wouldn't you rather be proud to have your children look up to Yankee greats once again?

Point #5: Join the Legions of Fans Who Demand a Salary Cap.

If Georgie remains at the Yankee helm, he will fight this tooth and nail. And as long as he's got a pushover for a commissioner who will do whatever is necessary to keep George and the other owners happy, baseball will hurtle toward the inevitable implosion that having only a handful of rich teams able to win a championship will certainly cause.

Point #6: Endure the Inevitable Players' Strike That Will Occur When the Salary Cap Is Instituted.

The Players Association must be broken on this point. And while we are almost always on the side of Labor over Management, this organization is not a true union. Since when do workers who average more than $2.5 million dollars per year need a union? Unions are for working-class folks like grape pickers, loggers, and people who work at Wal-Mart.

The players know well that a team salary cap will keep their individual salaries within reason (if an average of $1.5 million per year can be considered within reason), while keeping superstar salaries down from $20–25 million a year to a reasonable $10–15. And this is why they will strike over this issue: They're greedy. No one wants a work stoppage, but unless there is a miraculous turnaround in the stance of the Players Association, a strike must be endured in order for baseball to be made right again. So, support the teams filled with replacement players that the owners put on the field, and be quick to show your support for your ball club after the Players Association finally agrees to a team salary cap.

Point #7: Tweak the Luxury Tax.

The Yankees scoffed at the Luxury Tax instituted in the last collective bargaining agreement, exceeding the limit by more than $70 million dollars in 2004, more than the entire payroll of the bottom eighteen teams. And now, George plans to redirect his Luxury Tax responsibilities into funding a new ballpark. Well, at least he's creative with his accounting, we have to give him that. But if the Luxury Tax represents a fine for exceeding the posted speed limit, then George is scoffing all the way to the bank, as he is routinely cited for doing 120 mph in a 55-mph zone. And there is no judge to take away his license.

Also, we must make certain that slacker owners who receive their millions via the Luxury Tax are not simply lining their own pockets with the money, but rather spending it to improve their teams. These bottom feeders are as much a part of the problem as Stein. Remember, people, the goal here is to be competitive.

Point #8: Advocate That the League Get a Real Commissioner.

We agree with Bob Costas on this one. Baseball needs an impartial commissioner. The position of commissioner was brought in to keep the owners in check, to be a watchdog of their behaviors, not to answer to them or—worse—advocate for them. Although Bud Selig has done many great things for the game, he is not now—nor has he ever been—a true commissioner of baseball. As a former owner, his decisions have shown that he is compromised and that he has been unable to remain objective. The commissioner should make decisions that are good for baseball, not solely for greedy owners.

Then, Enjoy the Benefits of a Restored Baseball Universe.

If you've followed steps one through eight, welcome to the side of the good guys. Welcome back from the Dark Side of "the Force." Pat yourself on the back for a job well done. Now when the Yankees win the World Series (and let's be honest, they will still win it more than any other team), you can truly savor and enjoy the victory, safe in the knowledge that the best team won—the team that deserved to win because it operated the best organization under the fairest possible rules, and not just the team that was so rich it could buy and sell the bottom fifteen franchises ten times over.

Do all this and you will also reap the benefits that the Yankees of long ago reaped, the great teams that were loved by an entire nation. As of now, the nation is being force-fed a Yankee-rich diet, and the rest of us are getting severe cases of pinstripe diarrhea. But if you follow *Kevin and Josh's Eight-Point Plan for Yankee Fans to Help Save Baseball,* fans of every other franchise will no longer cry out "ANYONE BUT THE YANKEES!" every October. Rather, you will be revered as the conquering heroes, a dream that now only exists in your wildest and most insane light beer-induced fantasies. Good, honest fans from all over America might just say, "You know, I like how that Yankee organization runs its team. Those Yankees have the classiest fans in baseball."

We know it's a stretch, but just imagine it. How foreign those words sound to us now, but they don't have to. A few serious tweaks and changes and baseball will be able to proudly call itself the National Pastime once again. Support for your team would grow exponentially, for you were the fans who helped change the game for the better. You've witnessed the twisted evil that had become of your New York Yankees, and now you can do something about it. Demand the changes in your organization from within and rout out the pestilence in a way that honors the ideals that you profess.

Additionally, as fans of the other teams, we will do our best not to become that which we feel is ruining baseball. We will dissuade our teams from buying their free agent talent at ever-escalating costs and from abandoning the practice of developing their own players from within their farm systems. Because honestly, since we cannot compete with Yankee money as it is now, developing players from within is our only viable option. Not true with you. You not only compete but dominate this game. If things were more equal, who knows what the owners of any of our teams would do. None have been powerful enough to be corrupted by the power that you now possess . . . or should we say, the power that now possesses you?

So Yankee fans, it's gut-check time. Will there be more of the same, or will you demand change? If you choose to come back to the good side of the "the Force," we will be with you, working together side by side for the betterment of baseball. If you choose the Dark Side yet again, know that your franchise will be destroyed in the end, left in tatters, as will baseball as we know it. The choice is yours.

Sincerely,

YOUR PALS, KEVIN AND JOSH

Chapter Eighteen

An Open Letter to George Steinbrenner

Dear Mr. Steinbrenner:

It is time for us to speak frankly to you, if we may. We think that it would be best for Major League Baseball, for the Yankees, and for you personally if you had a change of heart and reevaluated the way you run your baseball team. You possess tremendous power in the game right now, and we would like to encourage you to use it responsibly and to help make the entire game stronger and healthier.

Let's face it, none of us are going to live forever. And while we certainly do not wish you an early demise, we would like to remind you that eventually baseball will begin a Post-Steinbrenner Era. When the game of life passed by Ty Cobb, Old Man Comiskey,

Marge Schott, and Schottzies One and Two, many people in the game feigned grief for decorum's sake but shed few tears privately. When Lou Gehrig, Jackie Robinson, Roberto Clemente, and Gene Autry died, people genuinely mourned and reflected on the lives these inspirational individuals had led.

How do you want baseball and its fans to remember you, George? As someone whose win-at-all-costs attitude led to the dissolution of the game in many small-market cities across the country, weakening the game, and leading to the rise of NASCAR racing and bass fishing as the new national pastimes? Or, as someone who had a change of heart midway through his life and helped make the game a little bit more competitive and healthier than it was when he first found it?

We know we're asking for a lot from you. It isn't easy for any of us to admit we're wrong. But why wait until you're on your deathbed to face the plain hard facts regarding your life's work? Just because Darth Vader and Lee Atwater waited until the last possible minutes of their lives to renounce their evil ways doesn't mean you have to as well. To borrow a phrase from the Ghost of Christmas Future, "There's still time for you to do some good in this world, you miserable wretch." Allow us to be of some service to you in this regard. Consider us the Ghosts of Baseball Future.

First, you need to realize that you already have more money than you will ever need in your lifetime, and that goes for your children's lifetimes, and your grandchildren's and your great-grandchildren's lifetimes as well. It's not the money that motivates you anyway, right? You're driven by the competitive fire burning within you and the desire to prove to yourself, to the world, and to the ghost of your disapproving father that you're someone to be taken seriously in the world. So be open to the idea that in order to prove what a shrewd and worthy competitor you really are, you might need to sacrifice a few dollars in future earnings.

Second, you need to admit to yourself that the economics of baseball have gotten completely out of control. The players make way too much money, and it costs working, middle-class families way more than it should to attend games. And you've played a significant role in this abomination of the game. Aren't you a decent human being at heart, one who believes in the American Dream, and one who believes that a hard-working father of three shouldn't have to take out a second mortgage to be able to afford taking his kids to a baseball game?

Third, you need to realize that in this era of astronomical player salaries, baseball has turned into the players' game and Corporate America's game, not the fans' game, or owners' game, it once was. Sure, we understand that baseball is, and always has been, a business. But it is a business based on a game. And aren't games supposed to be fair and fun?

Consider this: Your third baseman, Alex Rodriguez, is playing under a $250 million, ten-year contract, which equates to more money in its totality than most Major League franchises are worth. The Milwaukee Brewers, for example, were sold for $223 million in 2005. The fact is, A-Rod has more long-term security than the Brewers have ever had. Whether he performs or not, whether he's healthy or not, he's getting his quarter of a billion dollars. And this is a guy who didn't even own a World Series ring when he signed his contract and who hasn't won one in the four years since. Heck, he's never even been on a pennant winner.

Wait, there's more: Your shortstop, Derek Jeter, makes $19 million per year, also as part of a ten-year deal. To put this in perspective, let's break his salary out to a per-game basis. Derek Jeter, the *second* highest paid Yankee in 2004, made $123,337 per game ($19 million divided by the 154 games he played). George, most elementary school teachers in this country work about four years to make as much money as Derek Jeter makes in nine innings, or the equivalent of about three hours. For decades those teachers and the rest of the average, hard-working Americans have been the backbone of the game. Today, they can scarcely afford to spend more than a night or two at the ballpark each year with their families. They're being priced-out of the experience by the $60 seats, the $7 hot dogs, and the $6 sodas in flimsy souvenir cups.

Now, we know the new realities of the game are tough on the owners too. In order to fill the ballpark each night you need to put a competitive team on the field. And that costs money. So how do you pay for those huge increases in player salaries? You raise ticket and concession prices. As a result, the real fans are going to the ballpark less and less often, while each year more and more of the tickets are sold to big corporations that send their partners and clients to the games. Going to a game is a prestigious thing for these folks, not a passion, not a spiritual exercise like it's supposed to be. And the ballpark atmosphere suffers as a result. The little guy, meanwhile, is stuck watching the game at home on a basic cable package that costs $60 per month (a significant slice of which you also get). Hey, we understand, you can't broadcast those games on free TV anymore. You've got to pay the ballplayers, and you have to provide a dental plan for the ballpark janitors, and you have a family of your own to feed.

Here's the way it is, George. The average fan can relate better to the average big league owner these days than to the average ballplayer. The players have us both by the balls or, more specifically, the Players Association does. The union is so powerful that anytime whispers of a salary cap emerge, all it has to do is mention the "s" word, and the fans and owners go reeling into a tizzy. After a few months of posturing and conceding on other, minor issues, the players and agents get their way. Then the Yankees start throwing their money around again, while the other owners sadly shake their heads and the players and agents laugh heartily all the way to the bank— the bank that they suddenly own.

Here's a novel idea, George, or at least one that may be novel to you. The fact that your team wins its division year-in and year-out is not very impressive when you consider that you spend way more money than any other team to do so. Your team *should* win every year considering its payroll doubles, triples, and even quadruples that of other teams. Fans are more impressed by teams like the Oakland A's and Florida Marlins that can spend a quarter of what the Yankees spend on player salaries and still compete. Now, if the playing field were truly level, and the Yankees were spending the same amount on players as every other team, and if the Yankees then still managed to be successful year after year, you'd have something to be really proud of and we'd give you your props. You'd be proving that your team was a superior evaluator of talent and developer of players. You'd be proving that Yankee Baseball and the Yankee Way were superior.

Given the current dynamic that exists, however, the only thing you manage to prove each year is that money can compensate for the lack of sound organizational leadership and vision. You're like one of the island chiefs in the south sea who prove how great they are by dumping massive amounts of livestock, gold, and riches into the sacrificial fire while the poor folk sit idly by, begging for bread.

It's pretty tough to argue with the claim that the Oakland A's, to offer just one example, know more about running a baseball team than you do. The Yankees spent $1,831,683 (in player salaries) per win in 2004 (101 wins, $185 million payroll), while the A's spent about $648,351 per win (91 wins, $59 million payroll). That means the Yankees spent $125 million more than the A's, and all that money resulted in was a lousy ten extra wins. We say, give Billy Bean another $125 million to play with in Oakland one of these years (or the equivalent of TEN additional $12 million per year players) and see who wins the AL Pennant on a yearly basis then.

Anticipating your counter-argument, we suspect you will claim that raising the money that gives your team this kind of payroll advantage is part of the game. Sorry, but we're not buying that tired line. New York was the country's biggest media market before George Steinbrenner came along, just like it will be when that vein finally bursts in your forehead. The cable TV money and advertising dollars the Yankees generate are largely the product of fortunate geography and of the Yankee tradition that was built long before your dog and pony show arrived in the Bronx.

If you're really a man who is driven by his competitive juices, why wouldn't you want to test your meddle on an even playing field? Don't you want to prove that you can run a baseball team—from top to bottom—better than anyone else? Why not try to win the old-fashioned way, by developing talent, coaching your average players to be good players and your good players to be great players, and by building a team that actually plays together as a team. Until you give it a try, you'll never know if there's anything exceptional about you, or if you're just another fortunate son who has spent his life turning daddy's money into more money and buying success.

So, here's what we need you to do, George. Do an about-face, and instead of siding with the Players Association in the next collective bargaining session, stand strong with your fellow owners. Stand up to those greedy players. Explain how the NFL has a hard salary cap in place and a revenue sharing plan and how football is becoming the country's new National Pastime because of it. Explain to the Players Association how successful the NFL has been. Explain how every year a whole slew of teams that weren't expected to be any good come out of nowhere and make the playoffs because the talent in the league is so evenly distributed. Explain how players from all teams can realistically dream of one day playing in the postseason. Then show the players some pictures of Edgerrin James's yacht and

Terrell Owens's mansion and explain how the players are still exceptionally well compensated for their talents. You might juxtapose these pictures with some photos of the average school teacher's yacht or average fireman's mansion, and you might remind the players who it is that *really* pays their salaries. Explain that across the country NFL stadiums are full for nearly every game, because almost every game is a competitive one. There are no Tampa Bay Devil Rays on the schedule. There are no nights when only half the seats are filled because the game's outcome is practically a foregone conclusion because Mike Mussina is matched up against Paul Abbott. Explain to the players, George, how they're rich enough already, and how you've had an epiphany: You now understand that winning isn't the most important thing after all; winning a *fair* game is.

Spend less on players, George, and as a show of good faith to your fans, cut ticket and hot dog prices. Take the game out of the hands of the corporate raiders and give it back to the fans. If you find that you just can't stop bidding up those player salaries, then champion a salary cap to keep yourself and the handful of other wealthy teams in check.

Let's imagine what would happen if you actually made this remarkable transformation. The result would probably be another work stoppage, but hopefully it would lead to some real reform in the league's collective bargaining agreement when the game returned. Player salaries would be held somewhat in check, the talent would be more evenly distributed across the teams, and more teams would be in the World Series hunt each September.

What would the end game be for the Yankees? Well, they probably wouldn't run away with the American League every year, but that's not to say they wouldn't be successful. If you made savvy personnel decisions at the front office level and let your "baseball people" run the baseball operations, maybe, the Yanks would still give their fans reasons to be proud. Certainly their television and advertising revenues would remain strong, considering they would still be in the nation's largest media market and that every regular season game would suddenly be that much more competitive and meaningful.

And what would George Steinbrenner's legacy be? Fifty years from now, how would the world remember you? As a bumbling billionaire who outspent all of the other owners of his day to win a handful of championships? Or as a man who played a leading role in returning the competitive balance to baseball and saved the game in cities like Pittsburgh, Detroit, Kansas City, St. Petersburg, Cleveland, and Milwaukee? They would remember you as the man who gave the game back to the fans. What we're offering here is the opportunity for you to reestablish real Yankee pride and perhaps even save baseball across the country as well. You'd be a hero, George, much like Kennesaw Mountain Landis, the commissioner who cleaned up baseball after the Black Sox Scandal of 1919.

Yes, it's true that you're reviled by hundreds of millions of people now. But we believe the forgiving American people would focus on the contributions you made to the game in your later years and would remember you fondly. At least we know we would, and we'd make sure that our kids and grandkids would too. That's not to say we would ever root for the Yankees, but it's likely we would stop hating them quite so much.

We sincerely hope that you will accept the olive branch that we have tried to extend on behalf of the game, its loyal fans, and great traditions. We do believe that people possess a remarkable capacity to change, and while we also believe that it is never too late to change, we believe that sooner is usually better than later. So what do you say, George, can you become the champion for a salary cap that would keep the future George Steinbrenners of the world in check and ensure that baseball is fun and exciting in all corners of America?

The ball is in your hands, so to speak. It's up to you to decide what you're going to do with it. You can hand it to A-Rod, and he'll likely sign it and then sell it on eBay for $180, or you can take aim at Scott Boras and Donald Fehr and do a little headhunting.

What's it going to be?

Sincerely,

KEVIN AND JOSH

Bibliography

Our task was made more feasible thanks to the following books, magazines, newspapers and Web sites that we used as references:

Films

Damn Yankees, Dir. George Abbott and Stanley Donen. Perf. Tab Hunter, Gwen Verdon, and Ray Walston. Warner Bros., 1958.

Books

Vancil, Mark and Mark Mandrake (eds). *The New York Yankees: One Hundred Years, The Official Retrospective*. New York: Ballantine Books, 2003.

Thorn, John and Pete Palmer, Michael Gershman, and David Pietrusa. *Total Baseball*, Sixth Edition, New York: Total Sports, 1999.

Allen, Maury. *All Roads Lead to October*. New York: St. Martin's Press, 2000.

Berra, Yogi and Dave Kaplan. *Ten Rings: My Championship Seasons*. New York: HarperCollins, Inc., 2003.

Bouton, Jim. *Ball Four*. New York, Macmillan General Reference, 1990.

Castro, Tony. *Mickey Mantle: America's Prodigal Son*. Dulles, VA: Brassey's Inc., 2002.

Costas, Bob. *Fair Ball: A Fan's Case for Baseball.* New York: Broadway Books, 2001.

Cramer, Richard Ben. *Joe DiMaggio: The Hero's Life.* New York: Simon & Schuster, 2000.

Frommer, Harvey and Frederic J. Frommer. *Red Sox vs. Yankees: The Great Rivalry.* Canada: Sports Publishing LLC., 2004.

Goodwin, Doris Kearns. *Wait Till Next Year.* New York: Touchtone Books, 1998.

Halberstam, David. *Summer of '49.* New York: Avon Books, 1989.

Kahn, Rober. *October Men: Reggie Jackson, George Steinbrenner, Billy Martin, and the Yankees' Miraculous Finish in 1978.* Orlando, FL: Harcourt, Inc., 2003.

Kahn, Roger. *The Era: 1947–1957, When the Yankees, the Giants, and the Dodgers Ruled the World.* Lincoln, NE: University of Nebraska Press, 2002.

Lewis, Michael. *Moneyball: The Art of Winning an Unfair Game.* New York: W.W. Norton & Co., 2003.

Lyle, Sparky. *The Bronx Zoo.* New York: Crown Publishers, 1979.

Madden, Bill. *The Pride of October: What It Was to Be Young and a Yankee.* New York: Warner Books, 2003.

Olney, Buster. *The Last Night of the Yankee Dynasty: The Game, the Team, and the Cost of Greatness.* New York: HarperCollins, Inc., 2004.

Ritter, Lawrence and Donald Honig. *The 100 Greatest Baseball Players of All Time.* New York: Crown Publishers, Inc., 1981.

Robinson, Ray. *Iron Horse: Lou Gehrig in His Time.* New York: W.W. Norton & Company, Inc., 1990.

Shaughnessy, Dan. *Curse of the Bambino.* New York: Penguin USA Books, 2000.

Periodicals

Baseball Weekly / Sports Weekly, 1993–2004.

The Boston Globe, 1949–2005.

ESPN The Magazine, 1998–2004.

The New York Times, 1974–2004.

The Pittsburgh Post-Gazette, 1950–2004

The Seattle Post-Intelligencer, 1994–2004

Sports Illustrated, 1959–2005.

Web Sites

baseballlibrary.com

baseball-almanac.com

brainyquote.com

cnnsi.com

espn.com

mlb.com

nationalpastime.com

sports-quotes.com

thejournalnews.com

timesleader.com

ultimateyankees.com

worldhistory.com

yahoo.com

yanks-suck.com

Acknowledgments

Kevin wishes to thank his wife, Meghan, for her abundant love and support. He would also like to apologize to the many Yankee fans in his family but to assure them that this book was one that simply had to be written.

Josh wishes to acknowledge his Red Sox–loving wife, Heather, and all of his friends and family members who have supported his writing and shared his love of baseball through the years.

The authors would also like to thank editors Rob Kirkpatrick and George Donahue at The Lyons Press, the kindly folks at The Globe Pequot Press, and Colleen Mohyde at The Doe Coover Agency.

This is the second book that Kevin O'Connell and Josh Pahigian have written together. *The Ultimate Baseball Road Trip* chronicled the pair's visits to all thirty major league baseball parks.

Kevin grew up in the Pacific Northwest attending Mariners games in the Kingdome back when the tickets were easy pickings. He is a graduate of Gonzaga University and is a vocal advocate for the Zags. His first written work was a film, *Houses and Rooms*, which premiered at the Seattle International Film Festival in 1999. Kevin holds an MFA from Emerson College and teaches writing at Duquesne University in Pittsburgh, where he lives with his wife, Meghan.

A lifelong Red Sox fan, Josh has written for several newspapers and magazines since entering the journalism field in 1994. He is also the author of *Spring Training Handbook*, a guide to baseball's spring training camps in Florida and Arizona. Josh holds degrees from The College of the Holy Cross and Emerson College and currently teaches writing at The University of New England in Biddeford, Maine.